John Mark Caton, Ph.D.

Last
Call

Suicide: An Unfinished Life

Last Call - Suicide: An Unfinished Life!

John Mark Caton

ISBN: 978-1-7333130-3-2

Library of Congress Control Number: 2020901755

Printed in the United States of America

2020 -- First Edition

Published by Austin Brothers Publishing

Fort Worth, Texas

www.abpbooks.com

AUSTIN
BROTHERS PUBLISHING

To My Brother James Who Will Be Loved and Missed Forever!

To the People of Cottonwood Creek Church Who Walked with Me Through the Healing Process!

To Those Struggling with Suicidal Thoughts Who Need the Courage to Live!

To Those Grieving the Loss of a Loved One and are Navigating the Sorrow and Sadness of an Unfinished Life!

Contents

Introduction

Although suicide ranks low on the list of books I would prefer to write, it consistently ranks high as a leading cause of death in the United States. My personal experience of the pain associated with losing a loved one from suicide compels me to write as I join many others on the journey to healing.

According to the American Foundation for Suicide Prevention, suicide is the 10th leading cause of death in the United States. Suicide claims more lives than war, murder, and natural disasters combined. For those between the ages of 10-34, suicide is the 2nd leading cause of death.

There is a good chance that you have been touched on some level by suicide. I hope the thoughts found in these chapters lead to a better understanding of suicide. Hopefully, it will help you love and encourage those who travel the devastating path resulting from the suicide of a loved one.

The dictionary defines suicide as "the act or an instance of taking one's own life voluntarily and intentionally, especially by a person of years of discretion and a sound mind." Synonyms for the word, according to Webster, are self-destruction, self-murder, self-slaughter, and self-violence. The word suicide first appeared in its English form in 1643. The etymology of the word comes from the Latin *sui* meaning "self or oneself" and the English *cide* meaning "to kill or to terminate." Therefore, when I use the term *suicide*, I am talking about the intentional or purposeful taking of one's own life.

Today, suicide generates increased conversation because of traditional media recognition and social media attention. The act of suicide is not a new phenomenon. Historical accounts of suicide trace as far back as records can take us. Certain factors like diagnosed mental illnesses and substance abuse problems are highly associated with suicide. At the same time, the actual reasons for suicide are amazingly complex and varied.

Although difficult to write, I hope this book helps anyone contemplating suicide or who has experienced suicide or a similar loss. The chapters offer biblical and theological answers to some of the toughest questions surrounding suicide. I will offer some helpful hints to those who are contemplating suicide or recovering from the suicide of a loved one. I hope that through the sharing of my personal experience with the grief and loss of my brother and my response to my brother's suicide, it will steer people away from making the same mistakes I did while trying to navigate such a difficult valley.

I pray this book encourages, educates, and provides answers and direction for anyone contemplating or touched by suicide in any capacity.

Last Call—The Shadow That Lasted for Years!

Therefore, since through God's mercy we have this ministry, we do not lose heart... [8]We are hard pressed on every side, but not crushed; perplexed, but not in despair; [9]persecuted, but not abandoned; struck down, but not destroyed. (2 Corinthians 4:1, 8-9)

One truth that never varies is that life is full of both avoidable and unavoidable changes. Positive and negative, expected and unexpected, and foreseen and unforeseen issues and opportunities occur that detour the present and derail the future. A common adage is, some things we might never really *get over*, sometimes the best thing we can do is *get through them*.

Although I was accustomed to life throwing a curveball, walking through the suicide of my brother was the biggest game-changer of all. At the time, I was the pastor of Cottonwood Creek Church, where I had a front-row seat to watch God work. The once small A-frame church in the quaint city of Fairview, Texas, had experienced tremendous growth and relocated to a property next to a massive six-lane toll road, which carries hundreds of thousands of people east and west through North Dallas. From a pastor's perspective, it couldn't get any better. God was graciously using our once small church to share His Word to our fast-growing area.

When the church first relocated, the gym, used for fellowship and recreation space throughout the week, also served as our worship space for Saturday and Sunday services. The Master Plan was to continue in the gym until God gave us the go-ahead to build a Worship Center.

In 2007, the required funds to begin construction on the new Worship Center were in place, and the building process remained surprisingly on schedule. At this time, the national economy unraveled, but it seemed as though God's gracious hand continued to protect the church as we moved toward the completion of the Worship Center.

The quickly approaching opening date required many walk-throughs, planning sessions, and logistical meetings. No words can describe the humbled excitement I felt as I attended the final meeting with church leadership to plan the transition from our last service in the gym to our first service in the brand-new Worship Center. Personally, this should have been one of my finest hours.

When God graciously led me to this group of believers in 1995, my first sermon examined John 21, where Jesus sought out Peter and replanted him back into ministry after his infamous denials of Christ before the crucifixion.

<u>John 21:17</u>, *After denying Christ, Peter went away a broken man probably seeking the safety of a life out of the public eye on a fishing vessel. However, God had other plans for Peter that did not include being an unknown fisherman in the middle of the lake on a boat. In the text, Jesus asked Peter three times, perhaps corresponding to the number of Peter's denials, "Do you love me"? All three times, Peter responded out of his brokenness and shame of previous denials of his savior. After asking the question, Jesus instructed Peter to "Feed my Sheep." Then two verses later, Jesus instructed Peter again to "Follow me!"*

On Mother's Day in 1995, which was my first sermon as the pastor at what was then FBC of Fairview, I closed the message by committing to the congregation to always do my best to "Feed the sheep and follow Jesus." Over the years, through ups and downs that invariably come with ministry, focusing on those two directives often recalibrated my decision making and reminded me of what God called me to do. Yes, I made numerous leadership mistakes along the way, but as best I could, I taught God's Word in a way to feed the sheep and follow Jesus.

The first Book I taught from Fairview's pulpit was Ephesians. The focus verse for that study was Ephesians 3:20-21, which says, *Now to him who is able to do immeasurably more than all we ask or imagine, according to his power that is at work within us, to him be glory in the church and in Christ Jesus throughout all generations, forever and ever! Amen.*

I challenged our church to pray and believe that God could and would do *immeasurably more* than we could even ask or imagine in our little church. I joined in the challenge seeking God's will for our church, and I believed that God could and would accomplish amazing work in and through us. However, watching God change lives and families and see us eternally impact our community blew me away. What God was doing in our church was way, way more than I could ever *ask or imagine.*

Twelve plus years after those first sermons and a church relocation, we all had front row seats to see *immeasurably more* than we anticipated. The move placed us in a location with opportunities to reach multiple cities, and we wanted this new Worship Center to honor God and provide a place for people to worship God wholeheartedly. I could never have imagined this back in 1995 when I first preached those words to that small group of people.

The final touches of this meeting ended after 10 p.m. The pace and excitement of the evening distracted me from paying attention to my phone, but as I walked to my truck, I instinctively hunted for it to let my family know that I was heading home.

I quickly noticed something was different and honestly strange. While in the meeting, I had missed several calls from my older brother, James. Neither my brother nor I were big phone-talkers, so to miss one call from him would have been surprising, but missing multiple calls that late at night shocked me, and at that moment, I knew something was wrong.

I immediately returned his calls, and his first words were, "I Love you. I'm sorry for all the things I've done to you over the years and all the embarrassment I've caused the family. I can't do this anymore. I'm done." Then he proceeded to ask me a few questions that ended with him urgently asking for my forgiveness before he carried out his plan to kill himself.

No one is ever prepared for this conversation. No class, no training, no amount of wisdom or knowledge can equip you for this conversation with someone you love. He was not overly emotional or hysterical. He was drunk; however, he also seemed lucid, clear-minded, and determined. On many occasions, my family had witnessed James battle back from the brink of dark, difficult situations and overwhelming defeat, but he no longer had the desire to fight; he was *done,* and I could hear the *doneness* in his voice.

He was serious, and every fiber in my being knew it; he was going to kill himself. He asked me questions like, "Am I a Christian? Can God forgive me? Can I still go to Heaven if I commit suicide? Why am I a drunk? Why am I like this? Why do I destroy everything I touch? Do you forgive me?"

These biblical and theological questions were bearable for me to answer because I could respond to those questions as a pastor. However, the question of personal forgiveness was the one I struggled with the most. Sure, as a Christian and a minister, I knew the Bible verses about forgiveness, just like I knew the verses about the nature and meaning of life, eternal security, and salvation. Yes,

I did forgive him to an extent because I knew it was the right thing to do, but I had heard the apologies and request for forgiveness so many times before. I wanted to see real change in his life before I fully forgave him, and I told him so.

Truthfully, I said many things in the conversation that I wish I could go back in time and change. Good reasons and years of bad experiences with my brother drove my responses, but none of those reasons or experiences matter now compared with the brother I wish I still had. A sad, but true, fact of life is that the precious moments in time rarely provide second takes or do-over opportunities. I have been haunted for years desiring another phone call with my brother, but that was the last call. I wish I could somehow be more convincing, talk better, persuade better. Honestly, I wish I could do a lot of things with my brother over again.

James was tough, humorous, adventurous, athletic, and strong just like you would want in a brother; however, he also had another side, which was a unique mixture of mean, trouble, selfishness, and addiction. The good James always drew attention. On the athletic field, James stood out as the best player on the team. At a party, he was the funniest guy in the room, and at work, he was the hardest-working employee when sober. But, the bad James was always lingering just below the surface with his lapses into addiction that left him and those around him spiraling out of control as he self-destructed and dragged others down with him.

That night, James confessed he had been fighting a losing battle with the bottle for two weeks when he had not been able to function or work. His employer informed him that he was being terminated, and this rejection was the last straw for him. Although he had previously experienced episodes that impacted his job, his hard work and talent usually earned him some grace. His boss would usually count his down days as vacation or personal days, letting him return to work when he was able. But not anymore.

We talked on the phone longer that night than we had ever talked before, and I knew he was seriously considering taking his life. Following James' divorce, he moved to some property outside of town in the middle of quiet roads and empty space. I believe that living alone in this remote location was not an issue when he was doing well, but when he encountered a tough season, the isolation led him back to his addiction. We spoke about this isolation, lost family, failed decisions, and almost every other serious topic. By the end of our phone conversation, James and I had developed a plan for him to make improvements to his life and his current situation. We were going to work together to help him move, find a new job, and get sober again.

When we hung up the phone, it appeared that a small victory occurred, and a bridge had been successfully crossed. The difficult road ahead would require a lot of energy and effort, but I felt that this plan could work, and we could see a permanent change in his life.

After the mentally exhausting conversation with my brother, Jeana and I planned the steps, but when I finally laid down in bed in what was now the early hours of the morning, I couldn't sleep. I wondered if I should hop in my truck and drive to Houston to be with my brother before the sun came up. But I chose not to. After our conversation, my thoughts were all over the map. At times, I felt he was okay compared to the insurmountable amount of work required to move into the new Worship Center successfully. At other times, my thoughts turned back to the conversation with James and the plan we had developed. The church was counting on me and James was counting on me. I was a mess and honestly slept very little.

I woke up the following morning and went to the church. Shortly after, my phone rang, showing an unknown number. The sheriff on the other end of the line informed me that, unfortunately, just a few minutes before his call, my brother had taken his life.

My world came crashing down. All I could think about was the regret of not driving to Houston after our phone call; I tormented myself wondering WHY I had not said something different, smarter, or more impactful the night before, and I felt an unquenchable longing that I should have intervened sooner before he was at the end of his rope. My self-talk said, "This was all my fault!"

At this moment, my world came crashing down with me as the visible wreck in the center of the mess that life had become overnight. I sobbed the entire drive to Houston, where I would reunite with devastated family members and friends. I knew they would be counting on me to say and do the right things; they would expect me to be the strong leader that helped them navigate through this tragic event. However, my strength had been shattered by my feelings of failure from the previous night. When the time came to go to my brother's home, I couldn't step through the door. I sat outside on his porch and cried. For once in my life, I found myself like Zechariah in the New Testament when he found out his wife Elizabeth was pregnant with John the Baptist. The Angel looked at Zechariah and said, *"and now you will be silent"* (Luke 1:20). I cried in silence while a few close friends and family removed my brother's possessions from his home.

My silence continued at the funeral home, where family members made memorial and burial arrangements for James. Although it seemed only right that the "Pastor-Brother" would preach the memorial message, I did not because I could not.

Grief, guilt, and a sense of failure broke my heart, and I could not speak. I desired to communicate healing words of God's grace and mercy, but I could not. All I could do was cry and play that phone call over and over and over again in my head asking why? I clearly remember the funeral director looking directly at us and saying, "Right-minded people do right-minded things, and James was not in his right mind when he took his life." Although that made sense then and it makes more sense now, I could not accept it.

Seasons of despair cause people to realize and lean on the strength of others around them, and this was certainly true at this moment. My mother, who had been widowed at a young age, turned out to be very much like Naomi in the Bible. Having lost her husband years earlier and now her son, I worried about how she would respond. My mom responded with incredible strength, like Naomi turning her care to everyone else.

Jeana, my amazing wife, reminded me of Ruth, who worked side-by-side with her mother-in-law, Naomi, and exhibited the godly characteristics of strength and devotion. My sister, Kathy, had the wisdom and talent to organize the unavoidable events ahead. The strong, hard-working women in my family did the work when I could not. All I could do was cry in silence while the words of that final phone call looped in my mind, and the guilt of not driving to Houston overwhelmed me.

After returning to Dallas, the following Sunday was to be the first service in our new Worship Center. If there was ever a time when I should preach or wanted to preach, it was that first Sunday in the Worship Center. I was so proud of my congregation and so overwhelmed by God's blessings that I wanted to preach—but I could not!

If there was ever a message our congregation wanted me to preach, it was that day—but I could not. A respected pastor friend who had mentored me from seminary through this very moment cleared his schedule and agreed to be the guest speaker who dedicated our new Worship Center for God's glory and plan.

The memory of walking on that brand-new stage in the beautiful Worship Center will forever be etched in my mind. As I climbed the platform steps carrying the weight of the week, the amazing people of Cottonwood Creek stood in silence and clapped. I wished that I could have removed the overlay of gloom in the room from this day that should have been a celebration.

The congregation knew what I had been through, and the excitement that should have filled the room was replaced with respectful reservation and shared grief. All I could do was cry, wave, and mouth, "thank you." I sat in silence on the stage that morning listening to someone else preach the dedication sermon and thought that I should have been strong enough for my church and my family. I felt that I had failed on so many levels.

Moving forward, I acted visibly stronger, pretending as though I was pulling out of the mental and emotional fog. However, internally, I continued to be a wreck. I returned to preaching and performing my other tasks as the pastor. My outward appearance was good, but I was not doing well on the inside. Why? Because I played that final phone call over and over again in my head. I reminded myself that if I had driven to Houston that night, James would still be alive.

One night, a trusted, well-respected group of men in the church came to my home and picked me up. Sensing my silent struggles, they took me to a house where they let me know that I did not need to walk this difficult journey alone. Although I knew their sincerity when they extended an open invitation for me to 'let it all out,' I could not and did not reveal the depths of my struggle. In my misguided mindset as their pastor, I believed I should be helping them, NOT the other way around. So, my internal struggles continued.

Truly, Cottonwood Creek is one of the greatest churches on the face of the planet, and I am beyond honored to be the pastor. When other congregations might have impatiently judged their leaders, Cottonwood Creek supported, loved, and showed continued kindness.

Following weekly sermons, the gracious people of Cottonwood Creek continued to communicate support by sharing how they had been impacted, touched, or challenged by a point in that day's message. Honestly, I would walk away from those conversations surprised and grateful that God had used me to impact anyone's life positively in spite of my weakness.

The confidence in my call to ministry even wavered. I only focused on my failures and grief. Often, I would walk away from those post-sermon conversations with people who had been touched by a sermon hoping that God would give me a sermon that could help me. Looking back, I had preached the exact words I needed, but I refused to allow them to take hold of my life and change my outlook. I had become a "do as I say, not as I do, pastor!"

Although I looked fine externally, my internal struggle lasted several more years as my mind remained filled with doubts and questions. I questioned if I could or should remain a Pastor. After all, I had failed my brother so miserably, and I had failed the people of Cottonwood Creek for not dealing with the loss of my brother with more spiritual maturity. This emotional torment led to distancing myself from people socially and personally. It was, by far, the most painful season that I have ever experienced.

I have always been a "rub some dirt on it" guy. I often told others to be strong or toughen up. On countless occasions, I shared Bible verses with hurting individuals that I know helped them grow and lean on God through tough circumstances. In my mind, my situation was different because I could not make any excuse for not preventing my brother from taking his life. A simple, four-hour drive could have saved him. The facts were stacked against me. I have always been the type of guy who owns my failures—and I had failed on multiple levels. The weight of this failure was too great for me to carry, as it was taking a tremendous toll on my life and my relationships. I knew that something had to change.

That turning point started as a result of a few honest and strait-forward conversations with cherished people in my life. The first caught me off guard. My wife is extremely patient and loving, and she had a front-row seat to my pain, grief, and implosion. Early one day, she caught my attention by asking me to set aside time that night to have a conversation. At this time, we had four young children and she wanted the discussion to occur after their early bedtime. I thought about the pending appointment all day as I read on her face that the conversation was going to be serious.

That night she started by reminding me who I used to be: someone who knew how to smile, laugh, and enjoy life and family. She reminded me of the passion and confidence that used to be synonymous with my personality.

She pointed out how checked-out I had become as if I were watching other people live but refusing to join in. She essentially said it was time for John Mark to come back for the sake of the family.

Yes, I had been there physically, but I had not been there emotionally and joyfully for them. I had become hardened and isolated emotionally because of my grief and guilt. Allowing myself to be truly happy again didn't feel right. As Jeana talked, I knew she was right. Ironically, mourning my past failures and broken family was fracturing my own family. While I thought I was compartmentalizing my grief, I wasn't. My grief and regret were affecting everyone around me. It was time for me to come clean and ask for help.

How many times had I taught the importance of not walking alone through trials and not isolating yourself from others? As Solomon said, *Two are better than one, because they have a good return for their labor: If either of them falls down, one can help the other up. But pity anyone who falls and has no one to help them up... Though one may be overpowered, two can defend themselves. A cord of three strands is not quickly broken* (Ecclesiastes 4:9-12). Yes, like so many believers, even Pastors can forget to "practice what we preach."

My journey to healing began by fully opening up to a few close friends. One by one, I retold the events of the final phone call with my brother, the guilt for not driving to Houston, and the true picture of my emotional condition. And one by one, they reacted with sadness and support. They were sad that I had carried this weight alone, and they were supportive because they committed to helping me navigate the path back to authentic strength and joy. Reflecting on the situation makes me wonder why in the world I waited so long and carried the weight alone.

One particular conversation continues to replay in my mind. I shared my struggles with a close friend, and I mentioned that I was considering leaving the ministry. He said, "Don't do that because as long as I've known you, God's hand has been on your life, and you have made a difference in the lives of so many." He showed me that my thinking was not based on truth but emotion, and he counseled me that true healing would not come until I was open with the congregation about my grief and pain.

His years of wisdom and experience led him to believe that when I shared the burdens I carried, the pain would lift, and others could be helped. He reminded me that I had preached, "Don't waste your struggle; use it for God's glory." In essence, he reminded me that too many Christians and even pastors try to act like things don't hurt, and life is perfect, but in all honesty, pain was and is a reality of life.

I did not immediately act on his advice, but after gaining renewed strength and peace, I prayerfully decided to be transparent with the church. I preached a message where I shared my journey of grief and guilt with the congregation. Although vulnerability was not my natural path, being open and honest in front of the people who weekly looked to me for guidance was a freeing experience.

In fact, more people related to my struggle than to the perfect persona I was trying to portray. The encouragement and love of God's people at Cottonwood Creek gave me the confidence to 'use my struggle' for the benefit of others instead of hiding behind it. Now I'm willing to teach on grief and even suicide without pretending or offering shallow "rub some dirt on it" advice.

At that point, I did not know what I know now: that I would walk with countless church members through thoughts of suicide, that I would mentor people who experienced loved ones taking their lives, and that a majority of my police chaplain calls would seem to be somehow related to suicide. Yes, every one of these conversations and circumstances dredges up my painful past, God now provides the strength and the words I need for each situation. Now, the advice I give is no longer hypothetical; it is tried and true.

Although honest conversation with my friends and my church were crucial, coming clean with God was by far the most difficult. Throughout my season of guilt and grief, I prayed for God to remove the pain. In actuality, I had been praying that God would let me see that last phone call with my brother differently. I prayed that God would assure me that whether I had gone to Houston that night or not, the outcome would have been the same. But God didn't do that—instead, God reminded me of the words and prayer of Apostle Paul in 2 Corinthians 12.

2 Corinthians 12:7, *Therefore, in order to keep me from becoming conceited, I was given a thorn in my* *flesh, a messenger of Satan, to torment me. ⁸Three times I pleaded with the Lord to take it away from me. ⁹But he said to me, "My grace is sufficient for you, for my power is made perfect in weakness." Therefore I will boast all the more gladly about my weaknesses, so that Christ's power may rest on me. ¹⁰That is why, for Christ's sake, I delight in weaknesses, in insults, in hardships, in persecutions, in difficulties. For when I am weak, then I am strong.*

The meaning of that passage gained new relevance to me:

- I realized that my brother's suicide was my 'thorn,' and it wasn't going away.
- I realized that if a spiritual giant of a man like the Apostle Paul could have a thorn, so could I.
- I realized that when I shared openly about my 'thorn,' Christ's power worked through me to positively impact someone else's life.
- I realized that my weakness led to God's strength in me.

Now, when I reflect on my brother's suicide, a fresh perspective reveals the things I would do differently, including the phone call and the drive to Houston that night. However, I'll never have a second chance at either of those, but perspective also reveals some advice that could have saved me and others a lot of pain.

First, avoid isolation at all costs. Be open and honest with others about the emotions of guilt and grief. Second, remember that God's truth is the same before and after a tragedy, and it applies to you and not just others. Third, allow yourself to smile and enjoy the things in life that deserve a smile. Finally, choose strength instead of weakness. After all, that is what true living is all about—taking both the good and the bad that comes our way and letting God, church, and friends help you through it. So, "Don't waste your struggle; use it for God's glory!"

> **2 Corinthians 1:2,** *Grace and peace to you from God our Father and the Lord Jesus Christ. ³Praise be to the God and Father of our Lord Jesus Christ, the Father of compassion and the God of all comfort, ⁴who comforts us in all our troubles, so that we can comfort those in any trouble with the comfort we ourselves receive from God.*

What Does the Bible Say About Suicide?

"All Scripture is God-breathed and is useful for teaching, rebuking, correcting and training in righteousness, [17]so that the servant of God may be thoroughly equipped for every good work." (2 Timothy 3:16-17)

Suicide is an ever-growing problem in our world and every community. In the last ten years, the teen suicide rate has increased by more than seventy percent. Every school district surrounding our church experiences a suicide every year among its students and staff with the age of the youngest suicide getting younger and younger every year.

Like many other topics of our day, opinions vary, and emotions run high when discussing the issue of suicide. However, it is important for us always to let God's Word answer life's most important questions—and the questions of suicide are no different.

Is Suicide a Sin?

Yes, the Bible is very clear that suicide is a sin. The sixth commandment says, *You shall not murder* (Exodus 20:13). Just like murdering someone else is a sin, suicide is, in fact, self-murder or murder of self, which is also a sin.

God is the One Who gives life, and none of us have the right to take life, even if it is our own life. The Psalmist wrote, *My times are in your hands* (Psalm 31:15), and God ordains both the beginning and the end of our life. Solomon wrote, *There is a time for everything, and a season for every activity under the heavens: a time to be born and a time to die* (Ecclesiastes 3:1-2). So, suicide is a sin because it breaks the sixth commandment and ends a God-ordained life prematurely.

Can a Christian Commit Suicide?

Whether a Christian can commit suicide or not is a question that has been debated for centuries. Some believe that a genuine Christian would not commit suicide. Others believe a Christian could not commit suicide because God would not permit it. However, there is no biblical support for the idea that God would not allow an authentic believer to commit suicide.

If a Christian can commit any sin, why couldn't a Christian commit the sin of suicide? We see examples in Scripture of believers committing murder, adultery, stealing, lying, covetousness, and many other transgressions, and surely, if they can commit those sins, then a Christian can also commit the sin of suicide. If a Christian can murder and take someone else's life, why can't they take their own?

So, the answer is indisputable. Yes! Not only can a Christian commit suicide they unquestionably have. Being a Christian does not insulate an individual from life's most difficult trials or dark days of anxiety and depression. Individuals like Job, Moses, Elijah, Jeremiah, and others at times evened desired death more than life. Nor does being a Christian prevent a person from bearing the consequences of sin. However, a Christian committing suicide would never be God's will.

Can a Christian Commit Suicide and Still Go to Heaven?

Can a Christian still go to Heaven if they commit suicide? This question has been debated for centuries. The reason for such a debate is that suicide is a great and tragic sin with permanent consequences. Some religious traditions teach that if a person commits suicide, it is a sign that they have already lost their salvation. The traditional Roman Catholic position has been that suicide is a "mortal" sin and, therefore, would result in that person going to hell.

However, the Bible is clear that once a person is a Christian, they are a Christian eternally. Here are several biblical reasons that a Christian can still go to Heaven after committing suicide.

First, the manner of death does not determine one's eternal destiny. If a person who is unsaved commits suicide, it is not the manner of death that determines that person's eternal destiny. That person's destiny is determined by whether or not they have accepted Jesus Christ as their Savior. So, the manner of death is not the determining factor as to where a person will spend eternity.

Second, suicide is not an unpardonable sin. Those who reject a Christian's entrance into Heaven because of suicide are saying that suicide is an unpardonable sin. However, the only unpardonable sin is the sin of rejecting Jesus Christ as Savior. Jesus said, *I am the way and the truth and the life. No one comes to the Father except through me* (John 14:6). So, rejecting Jesus is the only unpardonable sin.

Finally, those who say a Christian loses their salvation by committing suicide do not have a biblical understanding of eternal security. If Jesus' sacrifice on the cross paid the price for any sin, why wouldn't it also pay the price for the sin of suicide? To say that suicide is such a bad sin that an individual loses salvation is essentially saying that one horribly "bad work or bad sin" can cut one off from Heaven. However, if salvation is gained by faith, how can it be lost by works?

The question then is, does the Bible teach eternal security of the believer regardless of whether that believer commits suicide or not? The answer to this question is found in Scripture alone and not philosophy.

Consider first of all the words of Jesus found in this passage:

John 5:24, *Truly, truly, I say to you, whoever hears my word and believes him who sent me has eternal life. He does not come into judgment, but has passed from death to life.*

Jesus promises that those who hear the Word and believe in Him: a) have eternal life, b) will not come into judgment, and c) have passed from death to life. Here we find an unconditional eternal promise from Jesus that if a person receives and believes, that person, at the point of belief, possesses eternal life. The phrase "has eternal life" means that the believer possesses eternal life the moment of belief. If a person has "eternal life" at one moment and then was to lose it in the future regardless of the reason, then it was not "eternal" to begin with, and Jesus would be a liar.

Notice also the words of Jesus in John 6.

John 6:37, *All that the Father gives me will come to me, and whoever comes to me I will never cast out.*

If Jesus Christ has promised to receive all those who come to Him and never cast them out, then it certainly reveals the glorious truth of eternal security regardless of the manner of death—even if it was suicide.

Look also at the words of Jesus in John 10.

John 10:28, *I give them eternal life, and they will never perish, and no one will snatch them out of my hand.*

First, note carefully that this verse says eternal life is "given" by Jesus Christ, and no one will be able to snatch the one who has received eternal life out of Jesus' hand. Again, if a decision to commit suicide caused a Christ-follower to lose eternal life—then they would have been "snatched" out of Jesus' hand.

The Apostle Paul adds even more weight to the doctrine of eternal security regardless of the manner of death in Romans.

> **Romans 8:37,** *No, in all these things we are more than conquerors through him who loved us. [38]For I am convinced that neither death nor life, neither angels nor demons, neither the present nor the future, nor any powers, [39]neither height nor depth, nor anything else in all creation, will be able to separate us from the love of God that is in Christ Jesus our Lord.*

Paul affirms that nothing can separate the believer from the love of God. So taking all these verses together, if a Christian commits suicide, they do not lose their salvation for several reasons: a) the definition of "eternal life" necessarily means eternal and does not mean until the point of suicide; b) no one who comes to the heavenly Father in salvation will ever be cast away—certainly losing salvation because of suicide would be such a "casting away;" c) no one who has been given eternal life by Jesus, will be "snatched" out of His hand—if Satan or depression leads a person to commit suicide which led to the loss of salvation that would be a "snatching away;" and d) nothing can separate us from the love of God—neither things in the present or the future. Therefore, if a person was a Christian before their suicide, they are in Heaven after the suicide.

Do Christians Struggle with Depression and Suicidal Thoughts?

In recent years, several high-profile Christian pastors, ministers, missionaries, and servants of God have committed suicide after long battles with depression. Certainly, throughout history, many other Christians have struggled mightily with depression and suicidal thoughts.

The two greatest Reformers, Martin Luther and John Calvin, both suffered from severe depressions and anxiety. John Calvin studied anxiety a lot in his day and gave much thought to it and wrote about it often. Calvin even stated that he was prone to it and often overate because of it.

Martin Luther, who changed the trajectory of Christianity back toward the truth found in Scripture, struggled with long depressive episodes. Some who have examined Martin Luther's life and writings believe he may have struggled with a bipolar disorder.

C.S. Lewis, the British Philosopher and Theologian most well-known for his immensely popular series "The Chronicles of Narnia," struggled with grief and severe depression after his wife's sudden death. He wrote about his experience with loss, depression, and grief in his book "A Grief Observed."

Mother Teresa, who is most known for her relentless caring for the poor and service to God, suffered deep depression and dark despair. At one-point Mother Teresa stated she wanted to smile at Jesus in order to hide her pain and the darkness of her soul from Him.

Charles Spurgeon was perhaps the greatest preacher of recent history and is referred to as the "Prince of Preachers." Yet, Spurgeon also struggled with long seasons of depression. In his 30's, Spurgeon developed several debilitating diseases that left him in constant pain and longing for death. At one point in his ministry, Spurgeon wrote, "I could say with Job, *My soul chooseth strangling rather than life* (Job 7:15). I could readily enough have laid violent hands upon myself, to escape from my misery of spirit."

Charles Spurgeon thought it was so important that he share his pain with others that he gave his preaching students a lecture entitled *"The Minister's Fainting Fits"* and said, "Knowing by most painful experience what deep depression of spirit means, being visited therewith at seasons by no means few or far between, I thought it might be consolatory to some of my brethren if I gave my thoughts thereon, that younger men might not fancy that some strange thing had happened to them when they became for a season possessed by melancholy; and that sadder men might know that one upon whom the sun has shone right joyously did not always walk in the light."

Many other Christians from history and in our present times struggled with or still struggle with depression and suicidal thoughts. The Bible never promises that followers of Christ won't have problems and won't have depressive or suicidal thoughts, but the Bible does promise that there is always a purpose to our pain and an eternal payoff for those who press on and don't give up.

How Do I Become a Christian?

This is the most important question anyone could ever answer. Too often, we complicate salvation and stray from its simplicity found in Scripture. Here is the biblical message of salvation.

- We are all sinners—

Romans 3:23, *for all have sinned and fall short of the glory of God,*

- God loves us even though we are sinners—

Romans 5:8, *But God demonstrates his own love for us in this: While we were still sinners, Christ died for us.*

- Jesus' death, burial, and resurrection paid the price for our sins—

Romans 6:23, *For the wages of sin is death, but the gift of God is eternal life in Christ Jesus our Lord.*

- We are not saved by being good enough or doing more good works—

Ephesians 2:8, *For it is by grace you have been saved, through faith—and this is not from yourselves, it is the gift of God— [9]not by works, so that no one can boast. [10]For we are God's handiwork, created in Christ Jesus to do good works, which God prepared in advance for us to do.*

- Salvation is a gift from God to everyone who believes in His Son, Jesus Christ--

Romans 10:9, *If you declare with your mouth, "Jesus is Lord," and believe in your heart that God raised him from the dead, you will be saved. [10]For it is with your heart that you believe and are justified, and it is with your mouth that you profess your faith and are saved... [13]for, "Everyone who calls on the name of the Lord will be saved."*

John 3:16, *For God so loved the world that he gave his one and only Son, that whoever believes in him shall not perish but have eternal life.*

- Salvation results in Eternal Life—

John 6:47, *Very truly I tell you, the one who believes has eternal life.*

John 11:25, *Jesus said to her, "I am the resurrection and the life. The one who believes in me will live, even though they die;*

A Simple Prayer to Become a Christian: "God, I know that I am a sinner and that my sin separates me from You. Thank you for loving me in spite of my sin and for sending Your Son to die on the cross for my sins. I believe that Jesus died on the cross and paid the price for my sins. I believe He was buried and rose again as the Scriptures state. I believe, in my heart, and accept by faith, Your Son, Jesus, as my Savior and Lord. Thank you, God, for saving me.

Suicides in Scripture—
Unfinished Lives

There are several very clear examples of suicide in the Bible and several other debatable instances of suicide.

JUDAS ISCARIOT-The Lust for Greed!

Judas Iscariot is probably the most well-known case of suicide in the Bible. Although most people correlate the name Judas with the betrayer of Jesus, the New Testament mentions several other individuals called by this name. Unlike today, Judas was a popular name during the New Testament era. In fact, another disciple and Jesus' brother shared the common name of Judas.

> John 14:22, *Then Judas (not Judas Iscariot) said, "But, Lord, why do you intend to show yourself to us and not to the world?"*

> Mark 6:3, *Isn't this the carpenter? Isn't this Mary's son and the brother of James, Joseph, Judas and*

Simon? Aren't his sisters here with us?" And they took offense at him.

Judas Iscariot was, in fact, the one who betrayed Jesus; however, he started with such great promise as one of Jesus' twelve chosen disciples.

Mark 3:16, *These are the twelve he appointed: Simon (to whom he gave the name Peter), James son of Zebedee and his brother John (to them he gave the name Boanerges, which means "sons of thunder"), Andrew, Philip, Bartholomew, Matthew, Thomas, James son of Alphaeus, Thaddaeus, Simon the Zealot and Judas Iscariot, who betrayed him.*

As one of the twelve, Judas Iscariot had a front-row seat to the life, ministry, teaching, healing, and power of Jesus. Bible scholars over the years debate whether *Iscariot* refers to a specific location in Judea or perhaps a group of Jewish zealots. Even though the exact reason that he was referred to as Iscariot remains unknown, we do know that the New Testament writers chose this name to specify him as the one who betrayed Jesus.

This designation as "Judas Iscariot" helps as we read the New Testament not to misidentify other men who shared the name of Judas in Scripture. In addition to being a betrayer, we also know that Judas Iscariot loved money and was the treasurer for Jesus and the disciples. Judas' love of money ultimately paved the way for the betrayal of Jesus.

John 12:1, *Six days before the Passover, Jesus came to Bethany, where Lazarus lived, whom Jesus had raised from the dead. ²Here a dinner was given in Jesus' honor. Martha served, while Lazarus was among those reclining at the table with him. ³Then Mary took about a pint of pure nard, an expensive perfume; she poured it on Jesus' feet and wiped his feet with her hair. And the house was filled with the fragrance of the perfume. ⁴But one of his disciples, Judas Iscariot, who was later to betray him, objected, ⁵"Why wasn't this perfume sold and the money given to the poor? It was worth a year's wages." ⁶He did not say this because he cared about the poor but because he was a thief; as keeper of the money bag, he used to help himself to what was put into it.*

Matthew 26:14, *Then one of the Twelve—the one called Judas Iscariot—went to the chief priests ¹⁵and asked, "What are you willing to give me if I deliver him over to you?" So they counted out for him thirty pieces of silver. From then on Judas watched for an opportunity to hand him over.*

It might surprise some, but Jesus was aware from the beginning that Judas Iscariot would ultimately betray him. So, the final betrayal didn't come as a shock or surprise to Jesus.

John 6:70, *Then Jesus replied, "Have I not chosen you, the Twelve? Yet one of you is a devil!" ⁷¹(He* *meant Judas, the son of Simon Iscariot, who, though one of the Twelve, was later to betray him.)*

Then in the upper room, Jesus again telegraphs for both Judas Iscariot and the group that He knows who would betray Him.

John 13:18, *"I am not referring to all of you; I know those I have chosen. But this is to fulfill this passage of Scripture: 'He who shared my bread has turned against me.' ¹⁹"I am telling you now before it happens, so that when it does happen you will believe that I am who I am. ²⁰Very truly I tell you, whoever accepts anyone I send accepts me; and whoever accepts me accepts the one who sent me." ²¹After he had said this, Jesus was troubled in spirit and testified, "Very truly I tell you, one of you is going to betray me." ²²His disciples stared at one another, at a loss to know which of them he meant. ²³One of them, the disciple whom Jesus loved, was reclining next to him. ²⁴Simon Peter motioned to this disciple and said, "Ask him which one he means." ²⁵Leaning back against Jesus, he asked him, "Lord, who is it?" ²⁶Jesus answered, "It is the one to whom I will give this piece of bread when I have dipped it in the dish." Then, dipping the piece of bread, he gave it to Judas, the son of Simon Iscariot.*

Judas Iscariot's final act of betrayal played out in the Garden of Gethsemane, where Jesus retreated with His other Disciples to pray after their time in the upper room.

Matthew 26:47, *While he was still speaking, Judas, one of the Twelve, arrived. With him was a large crowd armed with swords and clubs, sent from the chief priests and the elders of the people.* ⁴⁸*Now the betrayer had arranged a signal with them: "The one I kiss is the man; arrest him."* ⁴⁹*Going at once to Jesus, Judas said, "Greetings, Rabbi!" and kissed him.* ⁵⁰*Jesus replied, "Do what you came for, friend." Then the men stepped forward, seized Jesus and arrested him.*

As tragic as the betrayal of Jesus was, the events that followed this kiss were even more devastating. Just like with many of us, the shame we feel over sins or failures ultimately leads down one of two paths. First, one can recognize sin, repent, and cling to God's promise of forgiveness and redemption in Christ. Second, one can be overwhelmed by despair, lose all hope in life, and ultimately quit. Judas Iscariot's shame and guilt led him down the latter path. Following the betrayal of Jesus, his remorse and guilt consumed him, and Judas committed suicide by hanging.

Matthew 27:1, *Early in the morning, all the chief priests and the elders of the people made their plans how to have Jesus executed.* ²*So they bound him, led him away and handed him over to Pilate the governor.* ³*When Judas, who had betrayed him, saw that Jesus was condemned, he was seized with remorse and returned the thirty pieces of silver to the chief priests and the elders.* ⁴*"I have sinned," he said, "for I have*

betrayed innocent blood." "What is that to us?" they
replied. "That's your responsibility." ⁵So Judas threw
the money into the temple and left. Then he went
away and hanged himself.

One might wonder why Jesus would choose Judas Iscariot as one of His Disciples if He knew he was going to
betray Him. The answer lies deep within the love of God
and the compassion that Jesus has for each one of us. God
desires that none should perish, and all should come to
repentance (2 Peter 3:9). As such, God does not eliminate
any of us from His grace based on our sinful past, present,
or future.

The better question is why Judas Iscariot would betray Christ after walking so closely with Him for so long?
However, like Judas, people today continue to betray and
drift away from Christ, ignoring all that Jesus has done for
them.

Ultimately, selfishness and sinfulness cause personal betrayal and denial of Christ. Judas Iscariot had every
opportunity to change. I'll even submit that even after he
betrayed Christ, Judas could have repented and found the
grace and love of Christ. After all, when Jesus hung on the
cross, He said, *"Father, forgive them..."* (Luke 23:34). However, Judas did not choose repentance leading to grace and
forgiveness—instead, he sinned again by committing suicide.

KING SAUL—A Lust for Power!

Saul was Israel's first king. It is evident in Scripture that God did not want the Children of Israel to be ruled by a king. Instead, God desired for them to operate as a theocracy. Theocracy is the combination of two Greek words meaning "God" and "rule or government." A theocratic nation would be ruled by God, not by an earthly king.

However, the Israelites looked around at their surrounding enemies and noticed that every other group had an earthly king, and they cried out for one as well. Through Samuel the Prophet, God warned the Children of Israel about the dangers and warnings of being ruled by a king.

1 Samuel 8:10, *Samuel told all the words of the Lord to the people who were asking him for a king. ¹¹He said, "This is what the king who will reign over you will claim as his rights: He will take your sons and make them serve with his chariots and horses, and they will run in front of his chariots. ¹²Some he will assign to be commanders of thousands and commanders of fifties, and others to plow his ground and reap his harvest, and still others to make weapons of war and equipment for his chariots. ¹³He will take your daughters to be perfumers and cooks and bakers. ¹⁴He will take the best of your fields and vineyards and olive groves and give them to his attendants. ¹⁵He will take a tenth of your grain and of your vintage and give it to his officials and attendants. ¹⁶Your male and female servants and the best of your cattle and* *donkeys he will take for his own use. ¹⁷He will take a tenth of your flocks, and you yourselves will become his slaves. ¹⁸When that day comes, you will cry out for relief from the king you have chosen, but the Lord will not answer you in that day." ¹⁹But the people refused to listen to Samuel. "No!" they said. "We want a king over us.*

Therefore, the Israelites rejected God's plan for a theocracy in Israel, and God gave them a king named Saul, who was anointed by the prophet Samuel.

1 Samuel 10:1, *Then Samuel took a flask of olive oil and poured it on Saul's head and kissed him, saying, "Has not the Lord anointed you ruler over his inheritance? ... ⁶The Spirit of the Lord will come powerfully upon you, and you will prophesy with them; and you will be changed into a different person. ⁷Once these signs are fulfilled, do whatever your hand finds to do, for God is with you... ¹⁷Samuel summoned the people of Israel to the Lord at Mizpah ¹⁸and said to them, "This is what the Lord, the God of Israel, says: 'I brought Israel up out of Egypt, and I delivered you from the power of Egypt and all the kingdoms that oppressed you.' ¹⁹But you have now rejected your God, who saves you out of all your disasters and calamities. And you have said, 'No, appoint a king over us.' So now present yourselves before the Lord by your tribes and clans....'" ²⁴Samuel said to all the people, "Do you see the man the Lord has chosen? There is no one like him among all the people." Then the people shouted, "Long live the king!"*

If there was ever anyone who fit the profile of a good first king, it was Saul. He was tall, strong, and handsome. Even though God did not want a king to rule over the Children of Israel, He still empowered Saul with everything he needed to achieve success. Saul, however, was a troubled individual and leader. He lived his life constantly filled with pride, doubt, turmoil, and selfishness. Saul also jealously obsessed over a man named David, who God ultimately chose to be a better king than Saul and a man after God's own heart. Although there would be short seasons in Saul's life of repenting and desiring to live for God, his lifelong struggles always returned.

Had Saul lived a life of faithfulness to God instead of one of constant disobedience, turmoil, and jealousy, his story very likely would have turned out differently. As a result of his ongoing life of sinfulness, Saul lost God's favor, and his story ended with him taking his own life.

> **1 Samuel 31:1,** *Now the Philistines fought against Israel; the Israelites fled before them, and many fell dead on Mount Gilboa. ²The Philistines were in hot pursuit of Saul and his sons, and they killed his sons Jonathan, Abinadab and Malki-Shua. ³The fighting grew fierce around Saul, and when the archers overtook him, they wounded him critically. ⁴Saul said to his armor-bearer, "Draw your sword and run me through, or these uncircumcised fellows will come and run me through and abuse me." But his armor-bearer was terrified and would not do it; <u>so Saul took his own sword and fell on it</u>. ⁵When the armor-bearer saw that Saul was dead, he too fell on his sword and*

died with him. ⁶So Saul and his three sons and his armor-bearer and all his men died together that same day.

Just like Judas Iscariot, King Saul serves as a biblical example of a talented, blessed individual who chose to live life improperly focused. In the end, King Saul ended his life as he lived it by selfishly taking his own life.

SAMSON—A Lust for the Flesh!

Prior to the coronation of Saul as Israel's first King, the Israelites operated under a theocracy with God as their ruler and leader. We see this style of rule through the Book of Judges. During that time, the Israelites endured seasons of walking away or falling away from God. As a result, God would remove His hand of protection from the Israelites and allow their enemies to overtake and oppress them. Eventually, the Children of Israel would turn back to God and cry out in repentance.

God would then raise up a man or woman to deliver the Israelites from their enemies—the deliverers were called Judges. *Then the Lord raised up judges, who saved them out of the hands of these raiders* (Judges 2:16). These Judges would lead the people to victory and righteousness for a short season, but they never became the king. Once the deliverance was over, the Judge would go back to his or her community just as before.

This pattern of falling away from God, suffering at the hands of their enemies, repenting and crying out to

God happened over and over again in the Book of Judges. Samson was one of the final Judges to lead the Israelites back to victory. We meet Samson in Judges 13.

> **Judges 13:1**, *Again the Israelites did evil in the eyes of the Lord, so the Lord delivered them into the hands of the Philistines for forty years. ²A certain man of Zorah, named Manoah, from the clan of the Danites, had a wife who was childless, unable to give birth. ³The angel of the Lord appeared to her and said, "You are barren and childless, but you are going to become pregnant and give birth to a son. ⁴Now see to it that you drink no wine or other fermented drink and that you do not eat anything unclean. ⁵You will become pregnant and have a son whose head is never to be touched by a razor because the boy is to be a Nazirite, dedicated to God from the womb. He will take the lead in delivering Israel from the hands of the Philistines."... ²⁴The woman gave birth to a boy and named him Samson. He grew and the Lord blessed him, ²⁵and the Spirit of the Lord began to stir him..."*

Of all the Judges, Samson was a paradox. He was a good-looking, valiant warrior who was set apart to God at birth by good parents. His parents were seen as continually trying to point Samson back toward good decisions, right paths and God-honoring righteousness.

> **Judges 14:1**, *Samson went down to Timnah and saw there a young Philistine woman. ²When he returned, he said to his father and mother, "I have seen a Philistine woman in Timnah; now get her*

for me as my wife." ³His father and mother replied, "Isn't there an acceptable woman among your relatives or among all our people? Must you go to the uncircumcised Philistines to get a wife?" But Samson said to his father, "Get her for me. She's the right one for me." ⁴(His parents did not know that this was from the Lord, who was seeking an occasion to confront the Philistines; for at that time they were ruling over Israel.) ⁵Samson went down to Timnah together with his father and mother. As they approached the vineyards of Timnah, suddenly a young lion came roaring toward him. ⁶The Spirit of the Lord came powerfully upon him so that he tore the lion apart with his bare hands as he might have torn a young goat. But he told neither his father nor his mother what he had done. ⁷Then he went down and talked with the woman, and he liked her.

Samson mirrored the Children of Israel who were constantly walking away from God and choosing sinfulness. Regardless of how many times God showed him mercy and bailed him out of a difficult spot, Samson fell back into his temptation to sin. Toward the end of his life, Samson fell in love with the wrong woman named Delilah. Delilah did not reciprocate his love but instead sold him out for silver.

Judges 16:4, *Some time later, he fell in love with a woman in the Valley of Sorek whose name was Delilah. ⁵The rulers of the Philistines went to her and said, "See if you can lure him into showing you the secret of his great strength and how we can overpower* *him so we may tie him up and subdue him. Each one of us will give you eleven hundred shekels of silver." ⁶So Delilah said to Samson, "Tell me the secret of your great strength and how you can be tied up and subdued." ⁷Samson answered her, "If anyone ties me with seven fresh bowstrings that have not been dried, I'll become as weak as any other man." ⁸Then the rulers of the Philistines brought her seven fresh bowstrings that had not been dried, and she tied him with them. ⁹With men hidden in the room, she called to him, "Samson, the Philistines are upon you!" But he snapped the bowstrings as easily as a piece of string snaps when it comes close to a flame. So the secret of his strength was not discovered.*

Samson represents many of us today. He was at the wrong place, at the wrong time, doing the wrong thing with the wrong person. However, he managed to escape the situation unscathed. Instead of realizing the potential negative impact of dabbling with sin again, Samson, like many of us, brashly and foolheartedly continued to play with fire.

Judges 16:18, *When Delilah saw that he had told her everything, she sent word to the rulers of the Philistines, "Come back once more; he has told me everything." So the rulers of the Philistines returned with the silver in their hands. ¹⁹After putting him to sleep on her lap, she called for someone to shave off the seven braids of his hair, and so began to subdue him. And his strength left him. ²⁰Then she called, "Samson, the Philistines are upon you!" He awoke* *from his sleep and thought, "I'll go out as before and shake myself free." But he did not know that the Lord had left him.*

Perhaps no sadder words are found in Scripture than that last phrase; *he did not know that the Lord had left him.* God faithfully remained with Samson numerous times before and even worked through him in spite of his sinfulness, but enough was enough. After continually falling into temptation and making bad decisions, God finally allowed Samson to feel the consequences of his selfishness and sinfulness.

Judges 16:21, *Then the Philistines seized him, gouged out his eyes and took him down to Gaza. Binding him with bronze shackles, they set him to grinding grain in the prison.*

Up to this point, Samson had not fully experienced the consequences of his sinfulness even though he had played with fire more than once; he boldly and repeatedly sinned against God. Sampson received the grace of God throughout his entire life, but sadly, Samson began to take the grace of God for granted and assumed that he would never feel the consequences of his sin. However, sustained and repeated sinfulness has consequences, even for someone chosen by God.

But true to God's nature, even when Samson experienced the consequences of his sinfulness, the grace and compassion of God were at work. Perhaps unnoticeable at first, but rest assured the goodness and grace of God are always present and growing just like the hair on Samson's head.

Judges 16:22, *But the hair on his head began to grow again after it had been shaved.*

Repeatedly, God preserved Samson and even used his sinfulness for His glory, but this time was different. God still received the ultimate glory, but Samson's life would come to an end by his own hands.

Judges 16:25, *While they were in high spirits, they shouted, "Bring out Samson to entertain us." So they called Samson out of the prison, and he performed for them. When they stood him among the pillars, ²⁶Samson said to the servant who held his hand, "Put me where I can feel the pillars that support the temple, so that I may lean against them." ²⁷Now the temple was crowded with men and women; all the rulers of the Philistines were there, and on the roof were about three thousand men and women watching Samson perform. ²⁸Then Samson prayed to the Lord, "Sovereign Lord, remember me. Please, God, strengthen me just once more, and let me with one blow get revenge on the Philistines for my two eyes." ²⁹Then Samson reached toward the two central pillars on which the temple stood. Bracing himself against them, his right hand on the one and his left hand on the other, ³⁰Samson said, "Let me die with the Philistines!" Then he pushed with all his might, and down came the temple on the rulers and all the* *people in it. Thus he killed many more when he died than while he lived.*

Samson's life was indeed a paradox of righteousness and unrighteousness, temptation and triumph, but in the end, Samson saw no other way out than suicide.

The Bible also mentions several other explicit cases of those who were sinful, corrupt, or immoral, who ultimately committed suicide: Abimelech (Judges 9:54), Ahithophel (2 Samuel 17:23), and Zimri (1 Kings 16:18). Saul's armor-bearer (1 Samuel 31:4-6) also committed suicide, but we are told nothing about his life or character other than he committed suicide.

When reading these biblical accounts of suicide, take note that God desired so much more for these individuals; however, each made multiple mistakes and failed at numerous levels resulting in a final decision to take their own life. Jesus said, *The thief comes only to steal and kill and destroy; I have come that they may have life, and have it to the full* (John 10:10). Satan and our sinfulness only steals from us and destroys us, but Jesus wants to bring us life.

If you are contemplating suicide, don't choose Satan's path of death and destruction; instead, choose what Jesus wants—Life!

Courage to Live—The Promise of Future Blessings

He has sent me to bind up the brokenhearted... to comfort all who mourn... to bestow on them a crown of beauty instead of ashes, the oil of joy instead of mourning, and a garment of praise instead of a spirit of despair. (Isaiah 61:1-3)

Can someone who loves and serves God get to the point physically and emotionally of wanting to end or take their own life? Absolutely! Numerous examples can be found throughout the Bible. It is a misconception that being a Christian and living life God's way pardons you from ever experiencing seasons of doubt, despair, and hopelessness. However, real-life and the reality of living in a dark and sinful world does not support such a stance.

The Apostle Paul reminded the Roman believers that this world is filled with all kinds of difficulties and hardships. He wrote, *"Who shall separate us from the love of Christ? Shall trouble or hardship or persecution or famine or nakedness or danger or sword? ... [37]No, in all these things we are more than conquerors through him who loved us"* (Romans 8:35, 37).

The operative and often overlooked word in those verses is found in verse 37, and it's the word "in." Paul said, "in" all these things. No doubt, we wish Paul had chosen another preposition like "far from" which would have been much preferred. Even "around" or "near" would be an improvement over "in." However, the Apostle Paul clearly and intentionally used the term "in" to remind us that as followers of Christ living in a sinful and difficult world, we will encounter trials, trouble, and difficulties. Perhaps that is your experience right now.

Paul was reflecting a truth that Jesus shared with His Disciples before His betrayal and ultimate crucifixion.

John 14:27, *Peace I leave with you; my peace I give you. I do not give to you as the world gives. Do not let your hearts be troubled and do not be afraid.*

John 15:18, *If the world hates you, keep in mind that it hated me first.*

John 16:33, *"I have told you these things, so that in me you may have peace. In this world you will have trouble. But take heart! I have overcome the world"*

Biblical Examples of Those Who Considered Ending Their Life but Did Not!

Even those who love God and serve Him can despair of living and contemplate ending their lives. Being a Christian and living life God's way in no way guarantees one will not experience dark and difficult seasons in life. Several people throughout Scripture found themselves in seasons of despair even though they had obeyed God's Word and served Him wholeheartedly.

Job: It Doesn't Get Any Worse Than This – or Does It?

Most agree that Job's life was one of the most tragic stories in all of scripture. Although Job began his life in such a promising and faithful way, he suffered many overwhelming calamities.

Job 1:1, *In the land of Uz there lived a man whose name was Job. This man was blameless and upright; he feared God and shunned evil. ²He had seven sons and three daughters, ³and he owned seven thousand sheep, three thousand camels, five hundred yoke of oxen and five hundred donkeys, and had a large number of servants. He was the greatest man among all the people of the East.*

Job stood out among his contemporaries as a man who did everything in his life right. Spiritually speaking, Job loved God and shunned evil. As to his character, honesty and integrity marked his reputation. Relationally, Job's family portrayed perfection. Occupationally, Job succeeded at everything. Truly it seemed as though Job had the Midas touch in all areas of his life, and because of this platform, this man of integrity was the envy of the land and a model for others spiritually, relationally, and occupationally—Job was super successful!

However, just because Job lived well, this did not make him immune to the tragedies of life. A few verses later, Job's fortunes change, and he begins to lose everything.

> <u>Job 1:13,</u> *One day when Job's sons and daughters were feasting and drinking wine at the oldest brother's house, a messenger came to Job and said, "The oxen were plowing and the donkeys were grazing nearby, ¹⁵and the Sabeans attacked and made off with them. They put the servants to the sword, and I am the only one who has escaped to tell you!" ¹⁶While he was still speaking, another messenger came and said, "The fire of God fell from the heavens and burned up the sheep and the servants, and I am the only one who has escaped to tell you!" ¹⁷While he was still speaking, another messenger came and said, "The Chaldeans formed three raiding parties and swept down on your camels and made off with them. They put the servants to the sword, and I am the only one who has escaped to tell you!" ¹⁸While he was still speaking, yet another messenger came and said, "Your sons and daughters were feasting and drinking wine at the oldest brother's house, ¹⁹when suddenly a*

mighty wind swept in from the desert and struck the four corners of the house. It collapsed on them and they are dead, and I am the only one who has escaped to tell you!"

One can hardly imagine a more tragic scenario than Job. There are countless stories from the daily lives of those who lose their business or even family members. However, Job lost both his business and family in a matter of moments. Job's response to these calamities was completely natural. Job was overwhelmed with the emotions and responded in unquenchable grief.

Job 1:20, *At this, Job got up and tore his robe and shaved his head. Then he fell to the ground in worship ²¹and said: "Naked I came from my mother's womb, and naked I will depart. The Lord gave and the Lord has taken away; may the name of the Lord be praised." ²²In all this, Job did not sin by charging God with wrongdoing.*

Job responded just like we all would by grieving both inwardly and outwardly. He acknowledged that he did not bring anything into this world, and he ultimately would not take anything out of this world. Even through his grief, Job's amazing character and commitment to God comes shining through as he praised God instead of cursing him.

At this point, Job's spiritual commitment and integrity remained intact, but he was not finished experiencing life's losses. Job had lost his business and his children, but he still retained his health and wife, but that would soon change.

> **Job 2:7,** *...Job with painful sores from the soles of his feet to the crown of his head. *8*Then Job took a piece of broken pottery and scraped himself with it as he sat among the ashes. *9*His wife said to him, "Are you still maintaining your integrity? Curse God and die!"* *10*He replied, "You are talking like a foolish woman. Shall we accept good from God, and not trouble?"*

Next, Job's health and wife are both stripped from him as well. First, Job lost his health, and the imagery is almost too graphic. His body was covered with sores from the bottom of his feet to the crown of his head. The pain and pressure from those sores were so great that it felt better for Job to use pieces of broken pottery and lance his wounds.

What else could Job possibly lose? His business, his children, and now his health were all gone, but he still had the encouragement of his loving wife. However, even that now changes. The once-supportive wife who partnered with Job as his business and possessions grew, who gave birth to his children, and marveled at his physical strength and business acumen now looked at a broken man and suggested that Job take his own life.

Certainly, from an outside perspective, it would be difficult to think of a more hurtful suggestion for one spouse to give to another. After sharing many memories and celebrating so many victories together, the person Job trusted the most looked at his present state and essentially said, "You have nothing to live for!"

One can only imagine the depths of Job's loneliness and despair. But even in these overwhelming circumstances, Scripture says, *In all this, Job did not sin in what he said* (Job 1:10). Job held his tongue because he understood that losing it with his mouth would not improve his situation in the least, which would be a good lesson for each of us to learn during life's tribulations. Holding one's tongue is often praised in Scripture as an act of spiritual discipline.

Proverbs 10:19, *Sin is not ended by multiplying words, but the prudent hold their tongues.*

Proverbs 15:28, *The heart of the righteous weighs its answers, but the mouth of the wicked gushes evil.*

Proverbs 21:23, *Those who guard their mouths and their tongues keep themselves from calamity.*

While Job did not sin in what he said, we can only wonder what he thought or felt. After losing his wealth and health, surely Job hopelessly thought that life could not get worse. Job lost his family and faced the stark reality of never again experiencing their words of love and hugs. Then add to that the isolation he must have felt from the emotional abandonment from the spouse he loved. At this point, where could Job go for security, support, and encouragement? Could it get any worse?

Perhaps Job could count on his friends for solace.

Job 2:11, *When Job's three friends, Eliphaz the Temanite, Bildad the Shuhite and Zophar the Naamathite, heard about all the troubles that had come upon him, they set out from their homes and met together by agreement to go and sympathize with him and comfort him. [12]When they saw him from a distance, they could hardly recognize him; they began to weep aloud, and they tore their robes and sprinkled dust on their heads. [13]Then they sat on the ground with him for seven days and seven nights. No one said a word to him, because they saw how great his suffering was.*

Although Job's friends' responses to his problems were not perfect, they should be praised for what they did right at first. These initial actions can instruct us in how we should respond to a friend experiencing such an incredible loss.

First, Job's friends showed up! After hearing about his troubles, they set out from their homes to be present with Job in his season of despair. They were willing to set aside their priorities to invest in someone they loved. Secondly, Job's friends sympathized with him. When they first saw Job, life's difficulties weighed heavily on him, and his brokenness made him almost unrecognizable to them. Instead of suggesting that he clean himself up and get it together, they tore their own clothes and began to weep aloud with him sympathetically. The Bible tells us they took notice of how much he was suffering. Finally, upon first seeing Job, they did not offer unbeneficial, pious platitudes or hollow words of encouragement. The Bible says the friends sat on the ground with him for seven days and seven nights without saying a word.

However, the three friends did not remain silent forever, and when they did begin to speak, they only made the situation worse. In the Book of Job chapters 4-15, the friends offered their personal opinions on why God might have allowed such suffering to come upon Job. They asserted again and again that Job should repent and confess his wrongdoing that brought such tragic circumstances his way. When Job asserted that he was innocent of evil, his friends persisted in condemning him and suggested that he was the cause of God's divine judgment on him. They emphatically urged him to repent.

The example of the advice given by these three friends ought to cause us to pause before we ever attempt to speak for God. In essence, by condemning Job, the friends were trying to justify or defend God for allowing Job's suffering. His companions tried to point the finger at Job by accusing him of doing something wrong. They wrongly attempted to speak for God, saying that unless Job was guilty of something, God would never have allowed these misfortunes in his life. In their misguided and hollow words, the friends reversed all the good they had accomplished by showing up and sympathizing with Job's pain and suffering.

This message serves as a good reminder to each of us as we speak with those who are suffering. Since none of us knows God's purpose for allowing specific instances of

58 • Last Call

suffering, the best option we have is to quietly avoid sinning and causing further damage by giving untrue, harmful advice.

Finally, when God couldn't take the friends ramblings and misstatements any longer, he stepped in for Job and said, *After the Lord had said these things to Job, he said to Eliphaz the Temanite, "I am angry with you and your two friends, because you have not spoken the truth about me, as my servant Job has"* (Job 42:7).

Granted, in the end, Job does confess that he was not as holy and righteous as he had previously stated. However, Job truly had not committed the evil acts that had brought about his suffering. Job's friends were wrong! Job was a victim of bad circumstances and not a man being judged for his hidden sins, and in the end, Job actually prays for his misguided friends. God hears Job's prayer and chooses not to punish his friends for their misrepresentation of God and His ways. Then Scripture tells us:

> **Job 42:10,** *After Job had prayed for his friends, the Lord restored his fortunes and gave him twice as much as he had before. ¹¹All his brothers and sisters and everyone who had known him before came and ate with him in his house. They comforted and consoled him over all the trouble the Lord had brought on him, and each one gave him a piece of silver and a gold ring. ¹²The Lord blessed the latter part of Job's life more than the former part.*

Job is a great lesson for everyone who might consider taking their own life when they encounter financial, personal, relational, or physical loss. Had Job taken his life after successive tragedies, he would not have experienced the blessing of God's ultimate victory in his life. Remember, Job, in a very real sense, *"sat among the ashes"* of brokenness. If there was ever an individual who had a reason to end his life, it was Job. But Job had the courage to live through his difficulties and after hanging on and refusing to take his own life, he celebrated an amazing future filled with God's blessing and joy in life.

If you find yourself in a season of loss or someone you know is there and considering suicide, share Job's story with them accurately from beginning to end. Job lost everything, suffered greatly, felt abandoned by God, his spouse and then his friends did more to hurt than help. However, Job pressed on not giving up, quitting or taking his own life and he found a future filled with new joy and the blessings of God because he dared to live.

Elijah – It Doesn't Take Long to Go From the Mountain Top to the Valley!

Elijah is another example of someone who served God wholeheartedly but still experienced depression and despair to the point of wanting to end his own life. Elijah was an Old Testament prophet who lived in tumultuous times in Israel. He served God during the time of Ahab and Jezebel, the worst King and Queen of Israel's history. Two bookend verses tell us all we need to know about Ahab and Jezebel:

1 Kings 16:33, *Ahab did more to provoke the LORD, the God of Israel, to anger than all the kings of Israel who were before him.*

1 Kings 21:25, *There was none who sold himself to do what was evil in the sight of the LORD like Ahab, whom Jezebel his wife incited.*

Ahab and Jezebel steered the Israelite's to worship Baal and not the one true God. It was the Prophet Elijah who stood against the King and Queen's evil practices and ultimately led the Children of Israel back to God. From a casual reading from James 5, one might think that Elijah's life was filled with a flawless faithfulness to God.

James 5:16, *...The prayer of a righteous person is powerful and effective. [17]Elijah was a human being, even as we are. He prayed earnestly that it would not rain, and it did not rain on the land for three and a half years. [18]Again he prayed, and the heavens gave rain, and the earth produced its crops.*

Elijah was faithful, righteous, powerful, and effective. But don't overlook that phrase, "Elijah was a human being, even as we are." Elijah's life and ministry were marked by spiritual victory and defeat, success and failure, courage and fear, and emotional highs and despondent lows. At one point in his life, Elijah desired death more than life and prayed, *...I have had enough, Lord...take my life...* (1 Kings 19:4).

One might think that perhaps Elijah prayed for death after an agonizing defeat or loss similar to Job's, but that was not the case. Elijah's prayer for death took place after a literal mountain top experience.

Queen Jezebel was a Sidonian woman and a devout worshipper of Baal. She despised the prophets of God and encouraged her husband to build an altar to Baal and erect an Asherah Pole in the capital city of Samaria. An Asherah pole was a sacred pole built to honor a pagan god. Then she encouraged the king to kill the true prophets of God. In response to Ahab and Jezebel's rebellion against God, Elijah called for God's divine judgment to come upon Israel by praying *As the Lord, the God of Israel, lives, whom I serve, there will be neither dew nor rain in the next few years except at my word* (1 Kings 17:1).

Israel was an agrarian society, and as you might imagine, a drought would destroy the land and economy of the day. That prayer made Elijah a hated and wanted man in the king and queen's eyes. After three years, God told Elijah to go and present himself to the king, and then God would again bring rain on the land. Completely trusting God, Elijah demonstrated faithful courage by presenting himself before his enemy, *Elijah went to present himself to Ahab* (1 Kings 18:1).

Elijah approached the king and challenged him to an epic battle between God and Baal on a mountain called Carmel. The people of Israel and all the false prophets of Baal assembled on the mountain, and Elijah issued a challenge to the people saying:

1 Kings 18:23, *"Get two bulls for us. Let Baal's prophets choose one for themselves, and let them cut it into pieces and put it on the wood but not set fire to it. I will prepare the other bull and put it on the wood but not set fire to it. ²⁴Then you call on the name of your god, and I will call on the name of the Lord. The god who answers by fire—he is God." Then all the people said, "What you say is good."*

The prophets of Baal went first and built their altar and prayed, danced, and cut themselves, hoping Baal would show up, but to no avail and Scripture says, *...there was no response, no one answered, no one paid attention* (1 Kings 18:29).

Next up was Elijah and his One True God. Elijah built his altar, arranged the wood, and poured water on it not just once or twice but three times. Then Elijah prayed:

1 Kings 18:37, *Answer me, LORD, answer me, so these people will know that you, LORD, are God, and that you are turning their hearts back again." ³⁸Then the fire of the LORD fell and burned up the sacrifice, the wood, the stones and the soil, and also licked up the water in the trench. ³⁹When all the people saw this, they fell prostrate and cried, "The LORD—he is God! The LORD—he is God!"*

Even though the altar had been doused with water, God answered the prayers of Elijah and burned up the offering and demonstrated for all to see that Elijah did, in fact, serve the One True God. Then the people fell on their faces before God and repented from the Baal worship.

Rain soon returned to Israel, and Elijah became a national hero. It would be natural to think that after such a great victory, nothing could negatively affect or discourage Elijah. However, fast forward exactly one chapter in the Book of 1 Kings, where we find Elijah so disheartened and depressed that he would rather die than live.

How does this happen? Unlike Job, who had lost everything and experienced real tragedies, Elijah alone drove himself to the point of emotional despair. No loss, tragedy, or defeat existed!

Instead, Elijah's downward spiral resulted from what he feared might happen in the future rather than what he had already experienced in the past. Jezebel threatened to kill him because of her embarrassment over the failure of her prophets of Baal on Mount Carmel. Rather than trusting in God with his future and boldly standing against this evil queen, Elijah was afraid and ran away to hide. He ran until he was exhausted, alone, and isolated from everyone else. Elijah went into a cave and threw a pity party.

As with most pity party's, no one else participated, which only made the situation worse. Although God still had work for Elijah to complete, this once-successful prophet pouted alone in a cave in the middle of nowhere. God knew very well that the more Elijah sat in the cave of loneliness, the worse Elijah's despair would become.

So, God decided to shake Elijah up by asking a great question, *What are you doing here, Elijah?* (1 Kings 19:9). Elijah had an answer, but it was an answer that was a unique mixture of truth, untruths, and half-truths.

1 Kings 19:10, *He replied, "I have been very zealous for the Lord God Almighty. The Israelites have rejected your covenant, torn down your altars, and put your prophets to death with the sword. I am the only one left, and now they are trying to kill me too."*

Yes, it was true that Elijah was zealous for God and that some of the Israelites had rejected God. However, it was Jezebel and her followers who had torn down the altars and put some of the prophets of God to death, but not nearly all of them. Furthermore, the Israelites had repented and come back to God. Elijah's mind began to play tricks on him and he began to tell himself lies and believe them.

We would all do well to remember the negative effects of this self-selected isolation, which leads to feeling fearful, desperate, and alone. Beware of making this choice to avoid other people because throwing a pity party in the cave of our mental despair and relational isolation guarantees that no one will show up. Then like Elijah, we will blame others for abandoning us when in fact, we abandoned them. Often, others around us are ready and willing to help, but the one in need pushes them away. Ironically, this isolation often results in blaming others for the abandonment instead of seeing the real truth of the issue and the part we played in it.

How did Elijah pull out of his despair? He listened to God.

1 Kings 19:15, *"Go back the way you came... When you get there, anoint Hazael king over Aram. ¹⁶Also,*

anoint Jehu son of Nimshi king over Israel, and anoint
Elisha son of Shaphat from Abel Meholah to succeed
you as prophet... [18]*Yet I reserve seven thousand in*
Israel—all whose knees have not bowed down to Baal
and whose mouths have not kissed him."

In this text, God provided several steps to healing and
corrected a lie Elijah was telling himself: *Go Back, Anoint,*
and *yet I reserve seven thousand in Israel.* In the phrase *go*
back, God told Elijah to go back to people and stop isolating himself. Although isolation is often a natural human
response when facing discouragement, despair, and even
fear, it is one of the worst possible reactions we can have.
Being alone and isolating ourselves during seasons of discouragement often leads to listening to the negative self-
talk that led to the struggles. Extended isolation causes the
lies to grow louder and louder, with no voice-of-wisdom
around to redirect false-thinking.

God also told Elijah to *anoint* certain individuals to
positions of leadership. The word "anoint" points to a second key to overcoming problems of personal despair or
sadness. In the Old Testament, a shepherd would anoint
the sheep with oil to keep the insects from burrowing or
digging into the wool. The shepherd anointed the sheep
for the sheep's benefit and not the shepherds. When ap-
plied to people, the word means to "bless or encourage"
others to fulfill God's call in their lives. In other words,
the anointing of others is for their benefit and not our
own—anointing others is an unselfish act and requires us
to focus on other people.

To anoint someone requires focusing on others instead of self. One of the best things to do when you are feeling down is to turn the inward and destructive thoughts outward in order to bless and encourage other people. If all we ever desire is for others to meet our needs or join us in our misery and pain, we will not improve. Eventually, we will find ourselves isolated and alone not by choice but because others have moved on, given up, or respected the demand for space. However, encouraging and blessing others leads to healthy friendships and relationships and lifts our mood tremendously by taking our focus off of self and putting it on others.

Finally, God said, "Yet I reserve seven thousand in Israel." This might seem like an odd part of the healing process of emotional despair, but it is essential to understand. Part of Elijah's problem was that he thought he was the only person who loved God and encountered struggles— Elijah believed his own lies. Too often, we do the same. We believe that everyone else who loves God is happy and problem-free; however, nothing could be further from the truth. Everyone has problems, but not everyone handles their difficulties in the same manner. The method in which we tackle problems can, in fact, determine our perspective and happiness.

Why is this? How can people endure similar trials with different outlooks? Some come through trials stronger and closer to God, while others push God away and hold on to pain and suffering as if they were required accessories.

Perhaps the difference lies in the fact that some spend their time being with others "go back" and pouring out their lives to encourage and bless those around them "anoint" while others avoid human interaction and positive relationships. The simple truth is this—you can hide out in a cave listening to your mind telling you lies, or you can move past the pain to positively engage with other people for their benefit and eventually yours.

So for all of Elijah's accomplishments, he was "a human being, even as we are!" Elijah's spirit was powerful and effective, yet it was also discouraged and longed for death. However, he had the courage to live and did not take his own life, and he became a shining example of perseverance and pressing on through dark seasons of life.

God used Elijah before he desired to die, and God used Elijah after he wanted to die, and God will do the same thing with you. Had Elijah ended his life, he would have missed seeing the wonderful things God still had planned for him. The simple truth of suicide is: If in a season of despair or a horrible dip of discouragement, one chooses to end his or her life, the beautiful future God had planned is missed. Future plans, future relationships, future memories never materialize because life was unnecessarily cut short. Suicide is a permanent solution to a temporary problem.

Paul — Loving and Serving God Does Not Prevent Pain

The Apostle Paul exemplifies someone who served God with his whole heart, mind, soul, and strength. At birth, Paul carried two names: Saul, his Hebrew name, and Paul, his Roman name. Acts 13:9 makes the point that Paul's parents were both Jewish and Roman citizens and reveals that "Saul, was also called Paul..." Two names were not uncommon in those days to designate both the name of heritage and a name of citizenship.

Although Paul was Jewish, he was also a Roman citizen and could speak Hebrew, Greek, and Latin. Because of his roots as a Pharisee, he would have thought anything not Jewish was to be scorned and spurned. As Christianity grew, Paul's Jewish side grew more and more hostile toward believers. Saul was probably present at Stephen's trial but was definitely there when Stephen was stoned.

Acts 7:54, *When the members of the Sanhedrin heard this, they were furious and gnashed their teeth at him. ⁵⁵But Stephen, full of the Holy Spirit, looked up to heaven and saw the glory of God, and Jesus standing at the right hand of God. ⁵⁶"Look," he said, "I see heaven open and the Son of Man standing at the right hand of God." ⁵⁷At this they covered their ears and, yelling at the top of their voices, they all rushed at him, ⁵⁸dragged him out of the city and began to stone him. Meanwhile, the witnesses laid their coats at the feet of a young man named Saul. ⁵⁹While they were stoning him, Stephen prayed, "Lord Jesus, receive* *my spirit." ⁶⁰Then he fell on his knees and cried out, "Lord, do not hold this sin against them." When he had said this, he fell asleep.*

Paul continued to persecute believers and ultimately tried to destroy the church. In Acts Chapter 9, Saul aggressively sought to follow the Disciples and bring them back to Jerusalem as prisoners. He went to the High Priest and asked for letters to the synagogues in Damascus, so he could travel there and imprison men and women who were followers of Christ (Acts 9:2).

It was on this road to Damascus that Saul was blinded and heard Jesus' voice asking him why he continued to persecute Christians. Jesus told Saul to continue his journey to Damascus and meet with a man named Ananias. As a believer, Ananias was concerned that Saul was not the kind of man he wanted to meet with but was assured that Saul would be useful to the Kingdom of God.

Acts 9:15, *But the Lord said to Ananias, "Go! This man is my chosen instrument to proclaim my name to the Gentiles and their kings and to the people of Israel. ¹⁶I will show him how much he must suffer for my name."*

After his conversion, Saul began to use his Roman name "Paul" exclusively when he became the "apostle to the Gentiles." At first read, one might take note of the fact that Paul will be a chosen instrument of God. However, the word *suffer* enters the dialogue in Paul's initial call. In fact, he suffered to the extreme point of hating life. Paul listed his suffering in the book of 2 Corinthians.

> **2 Corinthians 11:23,** *Are they servants of Christ? (I am out of my mind to talk like this.) I am more. I have worked much harder, been in prison more frequently, been flogged more severely, and been exposed to death again and again.* ²⁴*Five times I received from the Jews the forty lashes minus one.* ²⁵*Three times I was beaten with rods, once I was pelted with stones, three times I was shipwrecked, I spent a night and a day in the open sea,* ²⁶*I have been constantly on the move. I have been in danger from rivers, in danger from bandits, in danger from my fellow Jews, in danger from Gentiles; in danger in the city, in danger in the country, in danger at sea; and in danger from false believers.* ²⁷*I have labored and toiled and have often gone without sleep; I have known hunger and thirst and have often gone without food; I have been cold and naked.* ²⁸*Besides everything else, I face daily the pressure of my concern for all the churches.*

This extreme amount of suffering proved that loving and serving God did not shield Paul nor does it shield us from life's greatest difficulties. You might think that a person of Paul's spiritual commitment level was immune to discouragement that we all feel when troubles come our way; however, it was quite the opposite. Paul explained his desperate feelings in 2 Corinthians.

2 Corinthians 1:8, *...We were under great pressure, far beyond our ability to endure, so that we <u>despaired of life itself</u>. ⁹Indeed, we felt we had received the sentence of death. But this happened that we might not rely on ourselves but on God...*

Paul openly mentions his suffering to the extent that he "despaired of life itself." However, even though he felt a desperate longing for life's end, Paul did not choose to end his life. He lived another 17 years, wrote eight to nine more books in the New Testament, and embarked on several more missionary journeys.

The powerful direction of the New Testament books of Romans, Ephesians, Philippians, Colossians, Philemon, Titus, and 1st and 2nd Timothy would have been missed had the apostle Paul taken his life those seventeen years earlier. Paul's courage to live and not give in to despairing thoughts allowed him to continue to make tremendously positive impacts on others.

Paul's example of being faithful to the end is what allows him to write these words:

2 Timothy 4:7, *I have fought the good fight, I have finished the race, I have kept the faith. ⁸Now there is in store for me the crown of righteousness, which the Lord, the righteous Judge, will award to me on that day—and not only to me, but also to all who have longed for his appearing.*

If you are in a season of despair, keep fighting the good fight. Finish your race with faith and encourage others to do the same.

Other Examples: An Unbeliever, Wasted Potential, and Misplaced Priorities!

In addition to Job, Elijah, and Paul, Scripture reveals several other individuals who considered death but chose against it.

The Philippian Jailor: An Unbeliever

Acts 16:25, *About midnight Paul and Silas were praying and singing hymns to God, and the other prisoners were listening to them.* ²⁶*Suddenly there was such a violent earthquake that the foundations of the prison were shaken. At once all the prison doors flew open, and everyone's chains came loose.* ²⁷*The jailer woke up, and when he saw the prison doors open, he drew his sword and was about to kill himself because he thought the prisoners had escaped.* ²⁸*But Paul shouted, "Don't harm yourself! We are all here!"*

This Philippian guard was not yet a follower of Christ; in fact, he was charged with watching over Paul and Silas while they were in prison for preaching the Gospel. The jailer thought that he had lost his prisoners after an earthquake. This caused great distress as he would be held personally responsible for losing those whom he was entrusted with guarding.

The situation was severe enough to cause the jailer to attempt suicide, yet Paul called out at the "right time" and kept the jailer from following through. This event led to the jailer's salvation as he asked, *"Sirs, what must I do to be saved?" They replied, "Believe in the Lord Jesus, and you will be saved—you and your household"* (Acts 16:30-31).

The result of the Jailor not committing suicide was that he experienced the grace of God and the joy of salvation. Beyond that, the positive eternal and immediate impact on his family should also be recognized.

Solomon: Wasted Potential

<u>Ecclesiastes 2:17</u>, *So I hated life, because the work that is done under the sun was grievous to me. All of it is meaningless, a chasing after the wind.*

Solomon was wise and wealthy, but he abandoned God's purpose for his life to pursue personal pleasures. As Solomon aged, he realized that his pursuit of personal pleasure had detoured his path from experiencing the true joy and happiness that comes from living a God-honoring life.

The elderly Solomon hated the meaningless, wasted life that he had built, but this king realized that he had the option, as do each of us, to learn from mistakes and make changes. He remembered the foundation of fearing God and following His commandments. As long as someone has breath, there is always the potential for life-changing help and improvements.

As a result, Solomon chose to let his failures be used for the instruction and betterment of others. His simple advice for success in life from this point forward was, *here is the conclusion of the matter: Fear God and keep his commandments, for this is the duty of all mankind* (Ecclesiastes 12:13).

Jonah: Misplaced Priorities!

<u>Jonah 4:4</u>, *But the Lord replied, "Is it right for you to be angry?" ⁵Jonah had gone out and sat down at a place east of the city. There he made himself a shelter, sat in its shade and waited to see what would happen to the city. ⁶Then the Lord God provided a leafy plant and made it grow up over Jonah to give shade for his head to ease his discomfort, and Jonah was very happy about the plant. ⁷But at dawn the next day God provided a worm, which chewed the plant so that it withered. ⁸When the sun rose, God provided a scorching east wind, and the sun blazed on Jonah's head so that he grew faint. He wanted to die, and said, "It would be better for me to die than to live." ⁹But God said to Jonah, "Is it right for you to be angry about the plant?" "It is," he said. "And I'm so angry I wish I were dead." ¹⁰But the Lord said, "You have been concerned about this plant, though you did not tend it or make it grow. It sprang up overnight and died overnight. ¹¹And should I not have concern for the great city of Nineveh, in which there are more than a hundred and twenty thousand people who*

cannot tell their right hand from their left—and also many animals?"

Jonah, the prophet of God, did not like the task God had assigned him. God wanted Jonah to preach to the Ninevites, who were a people group that Jonah hated and despised. So, Jonah went in a different direction and found himself in the belly of a great fish.

Eventually, Jonah did preach to the people of Nineveh just as God desired, and a great revival took place among the Ninevite people. Ironically, this resulted in Jonah being mad at God because he wanted God to focus on getting revenge instead of granting forgiveness, grace, and compassion to those Jonah hated.

Interestingly, God does not chastise Jonah for being mad at Him, but instead, God gave him an object lesson about his misplaced priorities. After the people of Nineveh repented, Jonah isolated himself on a mountain to sit and stew in his anger and bitterness. Jonah's isolation fueled his anger and depression to the point of wanting to die. God rebuked Jonah for his lack of love and compassion for those who had repented of their past deeds.

The story of Jonah should remind us that our prejudices and misplaced priorities can cause us to isolate ourselves from others and despair of living life. The more inwardly-focused we become, the more depression and isolation result, and the more we are unable to celebrate the grace of God in our own lives and in the lives of others.

Conclusion

These examples demonstrate that cutting one's life short by suicide is not God's will. Ending a life cancels the opportunity to experience God's future plans and purpose for His people.

- Job taught that when everything is lost, God can still bless the future more than He blessed the past.

- Elijah showed that the depth of despair and depression can quickly follow personal victories and success. Elijah also demonstrated that the best way to come back from the depths of despair is to bless and encourage others.

- Paul reminded us that choosing to serve God wholeheartedly would not prevent trying times; however, choosing life over death ultimately leads to victory and future opportunities to impact others for the greater good.

- The Philippian Jailor confirmed that even for the non-Christian, God never desires suicide. Ending life before one becomes a follower of Christ is eternally devastating and creates long-lasting negative impacts on family and friends.

- Solomon revealed that worldly pleasures never provide long-term happiness; his life also proved that God continued to teach that the true meaning of life can still be lived out and experienced, no matter one's age or stage of life.

- Finally, Jonah taught that misplaced priorities and hatred of others lead to loneliness and despair. Jonah also demonstrates that God is merciful and forgiving to all people regardless of their past sins.

These are all examples of individuals who had the courage to live through failure, defeat, desperation, fatigue, embarrassment, hopelessness, isolation, and loneliness. None of these individuals chose to end their lives, and all ended up experiencing future blessings and blessing others along the way.

So, remember Solomon's basic reminder to "fear God and keep His Commandments." Start now and take one step at a time in the right direction. No matter whether you are a student, young adult, single, married, or a senior adult, in your darkest days, you must press on. You may not be able to see it now, but God will use you in the future. Killing yourself is never God's plan and committing suicide causes one to miss the ultimate reward of having the courage to live—God's blessings.

Surviving Desperate Times— If You are Considering Suicide

We are hard pressed on every side, but not crushed; perplexed, but not in despair; persecuted, but not abandoned; struck down, but not destroyed. (2 Corinthians 4:8-9)

Common questions: Why Do I feel this way? Am I the only one who feels this way? What is the point of living? Why did I do that? Why do I always screw up? Why does everyone have more friends and more fun than me? If those questions sound familiar, you are not alone. These are common questions asked by a majority of people at different points in life. Sometimes these inquiries are asked jokingly to others in a very superficial way, yet other times these perplexing thoughts take place in the midst of deep, dark moments.

Familiar statements: I wish I were never born! I feel as though I have no purpose! I am just taking up space! I'm a burden to other people! I am alone in my struggles and my failures. Everyone has a better life than me! These common yet troublesome statements are usually made during a bumpy patch on life's difficult journey.

So, why are those questions and statements made? Why do people feel up one minute and down the next hour? Why can life be so messy?

The great preacher, Jonathan Edwards, delivered many great and memorable sermons. Interestingly, his most famous sermon is titled *Sinners in the Hands of Angry God*. When one is already struggling with thoughts of depression and hopelessness, why further add to the burden by bringing up God's anger? The sermon title reveals the passion of Edwards and his love for his listeners.

Jonathan Edwards was more than just an angry preacher; he was also a fantastic theological writer. He penned some of the most memorable books and writings in American religious history. Contrary to what one might think of a man who preached a sermon titled *Sinners in the Hands of an Angry God*, Edwards was also insightful, emotional, and extremely practical. He knew life and faith were filled with actions and emotions, thinking and feeling—the beliefs in our heads and the moods of our hearts.

One of Edwards' books, *The Freedom of the Will*, attempts to answer many common questions: Why do I make the choices I make? Why do I have certain desires that other people do not have? Do I truly have the free will to choose better for myself? Do I truly have free will to change my desires?

Edwards writes, on the very first page of *The Freedom of the Will*, "Therefore, I observe, that the Will…is plainly, that by which the mind chooses anything." That's pretty simple! To have a "will" means you have the ability to choose, to decide, and to do what you want to do *freely*. But it also means that what we do comes from what we want—our desires. So, our *will* comes from our *desires*—what we *do* comes from what we *want*.

This has significant meaning for those who are deeply depressed or even considering suicide. When people commit suicide, it is because they have lost their *desire* to live. For them, there is no reason to continue, to struggle, or to fight, so in that moment, they decide or desire to have death rather than life.

If you struggle with those thoughts and feelings, let me assure you it is, in fact, more desirable to struggle, fight, and live than to quit, but you have to will it and choose it. Your life matters to God, and it matters more to other people than you think. You have a God-given purpose that is still unfinished. You have a God-given dignity that far surpasses your current depressed state.

I realize that in your current state, you might not see or even feel like God has a purpose for your life, but He does! You may not feel like you have any dignity or importance left in life, but you do! Jesus told us very plainly that Satan, the thief, wants to take your purpose and dignity away from you. However, Jesus wants you to have purpose, meaning, and dignity in your life.

John 10:10, *The thief comes only to steal and kill and destroy; I have come that they may have life, and have it to the full.*

Three Truths about "You" from God's Word:

To fight against depressive and destructive emotions and thoughts, we must first look at God's truth to regain emotional balance. I pray that these three truths about "you" will reignite the desire in your heart for life.

1. God Created You in His Image!

Genesis 1:26, *Then God said, "Let us make mankind in our image, in our likeness, so that they may rule over the fish in the sea and the birds in the sky, over the livestock and all the wild animals, and over all the creatures that move along the ground." ²⁷So God created mankind in his own image, in the image of God he created them; male and female he created them.*

When God created human beings, He created them, and *only* them, in His own image. Both male and female are created in the image of God. Unlike everything else in all of creation, humanity is created in God's image—nothing else in creation is created in God's image. That means that you are special and specially made by God.

Being made in the image of God also means that we are far superior in our ability to think and feel. If being made in the image of God is not enough of a sign of your significance, God also sent His son into the world to die for your sins. You are so special in God's eyes that He desired to buy you back from a world that went wrong in sin.

No other aspect of God's creation receives the kind of love that humanity receives from God. Only humanity experiences the sacrificial, unconditional love of God. Scripture tells us that we love because God first loved us (1 John 4:19). Therefore, even our love for God and one another is first caused by the unconditional love God has for us because He created us in His image.

If you are reading this book, and you are not a Christian, you still bear the image of God. God's image is what helped shape and form your personality and every other characteristic in your life.

Whether you are male or female, rich or poor, educated or not—you still possess the image of God in your life. You possess inherent dignity, worth, and value not only in the eyes of God but also in the eyes of other people. The big question is that if we are created in the image of God and have inherent dignity and worth, why do we struggle and have so many problems?

The image of God has been marred and distorted by the Fall of humanity and disobedience to God—it is called sin. Back in Genesis 3, sin created fear, shame, blame, strife between people, and distance from God.

Genesis 3:8, *Then the man and his wife heard the sound of the Lord God as he was walking in the garden in the cool of the day, and they hid from the Lord God among the trees of the garden. ⁹But the Lord God called to the man, "Where are you?" ¹⁰He answered, "I heard you in the garden, and I was afraid because I was naked; so I hid." ¹¹And he said, "Who told you that you were* *naked? Have you eaten from the tree that I commanded you not to eat from?" ¹²The man said, "The woman you put here with me—she gave me some fruit from the tree, and I ate it." ¹³Then the Lord God said to the woman, "What is this you have done?" The woman said, "The serpent deceived me, and I ate."*

Since the moment where sin entered the world, those same realities of fear, shame, blame, strife, and distance from God greatly affect us today. If that were not bad enough, death also entered the world. Before the Fall, humanity lived in a state of sinless perfection and unbroken fellowship with both God and one another. Theologians and Christians alike have debated over the centuries about the exact effects of the Fall on the image of God in individuals. While no one fully knows the exact effect of sin on the image of God in our lives, we do know that we still possess the image of God in our lives, but it is broken and distorted by sin.

Indeed, even thoughts of suicide can be traced back to the Fall. Every mental illness, depressive tendency, even our anxieties and worries—all of them can be traced to the Fall. Theologians refer to this as the "noetic effects of sin." The word "noetic" comes from the Greek word *noétikos*, which means "thinking."

Romans 8:23, *We know that the whole creation has been groaning...and not only the creation, but we ourselves...*

So, sin not only affects our actions and relationships, but it also affects the way we think. The Bible says, the way we think about ourselves, the way we think about God, and the way we think about other people is distorted to some degree by sin. Everything from the body's chemical balance to methods of handling grief and struggles is all marred by sin.

Nevertheless, the effects of sin on our actions, relationships, and thinking have *NOT* destroyed the image of God in us—We continue to <u>bear</u> the image of God because we were created in the image of God. Therefore, regardless of how you feel or think about yourself, you still have dignity and worth in God's eyes because you were created in His image—that's truth number one.

2. God Created You for His Purpose!

Every single person with a rational thinking mind has asked themselves the questions, "Why am I here? What is my purpose? What was I put on this earth to do?" These are not only the questions of preachers or philosophers—they are the questions you, your neighbors, your friends, and your co-workers often ask. Everyone has guiding principles, thoughts, and values that answer these life-questions.

Christians believe that everyone is created for the same purpose, which is to glorify God with their whole life. Jesus said the following about the purpose of life.

Luke 10:27, *He answered, "'Love the Lord your God with all your heart and with all your soul and with all your strength and with all your mind'; and, 'Love your neighbor as yourself.'*

Loving God is not merely a rigid exercise of duty or command when love is truly and freely given and received. To love God means to treasure and delight in Him as your creator.

The point of the command to love God is not meant to create guilt for not putting God first. If so, most of us would feel guilty the majority of the time. The point of the command is that we should constantly try to prioritize God in the way we live, think, and act.

The second aspect of Jesus' statement about love is, *Love your neighbor as yourself.* Again, the point of this command to love others is not meant to create guilt for not loving others enough.

Jesus pointed out that life is NOT meaningless. When we lose our purpose in life, and our existence seems lost and pointless, refocus and remember that God designed us with a specific purpose to love God and others

Life is not meant to be figured out or lived out alone. We are not supposed to make up a purpose or solve problems on our own. God made each of us in His image, and He created everyone with a divine purpose to love Him and love others. We are not the product of a million accidents, bad or good luck, or good or bad choices. God created us with a purpose—that's truth number two.

3. God's Love Created You

As a pastor, I have questioned why God created the world in the first place. Why would God create a world in which sin would happen? Why develop a world where pain, evil, and suffering exist? Why didn't God create a world filled with constant perfection, with no pain, no problems, no evil, and no sin?

Many attempts have been made to answer these and other similar questions over the years. Some have stated that God created us because He needed us; however, a perfect God does not need us or anything else. If God needed us, then He wouldn't be God.

Others have stated that God created us because He needed people with whom He could form relationships. That's not true either because God exists in a perfect trinity of the Father, Son, and Holy Spirit. God has all the relationships that He could ever need.

So why did God create us? God created us not because He needed us, but because He *wanted* us. God is completely self-sufficient and self-sustaining. There is nothing we could provide Him that He does not already have. So, when we think about why we exist and why God created us, we must remember that God did not create us to fill something missing in Himself. Instead, God wanted us. God created us to share His glory and love with us.

If you struggle with depression, extreme loneliness, or even thoughts of suicide—feeling *wanted* is difficult to grasp. Remember, God wants you and loves you. This love does not require that you measure up to something special or spectacular to earn God's favor. Nor does this love demand that you, in any way, plug a hole in God and fulfill some lacking need God has.

God knows your every sin, your every imperfection, your every failure, your every fear—and He still wants and loves you.

Romans 5:8, *God demonstrates his own love for us in this: While we were still sinners, Christ died for us.*

Although it is difficult to grasp, God sent His one and only Son, Jesus Christ, to live the perfect life that we could never live. Then God's perfect Son died for humanity's sins, imperfections, and failures. My guess is that if you are struggling with depression and guilt of past or present failures, you probably have forgotten how much God loves you. You have probably forgotten that God loved you so much that He sent his Son to die for every sin and failure before you ever sinned or failed once.

Indeed, if you struggle with depression and suicidal thoughts due to overwhelming failure, worry, and anxiety, reflect on the words of Jesus from the sermon on the Mount.

Matthew 6:25, *Therefore I tell you, do not worry about your life, what you will eat or drink; or about your body, what you will wear. Is not life more than food, and the body more than clothes? ²⁶Look at the birds of the air; they do not sow or reap or store away in barns, and yet your heavenly Father feeds them. Are you not much more valuable than they? ²⁷Can any one of you by worrying add a single hour to your life? ²⁸And why do you worry about clothes? See how the flowers of the field grow. They do not labor or spin. ²⁹Yet I tell you that not even Solomon in all his splendor was dressed like one of these. ³⁰If that is how God clothes the grass of the field, which is here today and tomorrow is thrown into the fire, will he not much more clothe you—you of little* *faith? ³¹So do not worry, saying, 'What shall we eat?' or 'What shall we drink?' or 'What shall we wear?' ³²For the pagans run after all these things, and your heavenly Father knows that you need them. ³³But seek first his kingdom and his righteousness, and all these things will be given to you as well. ³⁴Therefore do not worry about tomorrow, for tomorrow will worry about itself. Each day has enough trouble of its own.*

Jesus said that God cares about birds and grass. He makes sure the birds eat, and the grass grows. If God cares that much about the birds, and if He cares that much about the grass, then Jesus wants you to know how much more He cares about you. God loves you more than you could ever realize or know this side of heaven!

In your seasons of despair or depression, don't ever forget those three things: 1) God made you in His image; 2) God created you with a divine purpose to Love Him and love others, and 3) God created you because He loves and wants you!

Practical Truths to Remember in Moments of Depression

Scripture not only helps to combat depression and suicidal thoughts; it also guides our thinking in those dark moments. Here are three practical truths to remember in moments of depression:

1. There ARE People in This World Who Will Help You and Love You

In moments of depression, the most common thought is that you are all alone, that no one is with you. If you are not already doing so, seek help from the medical and professional community. There could be body chemistry problems or concerns that need to be address, and only the professional medical community can effectively treat those.

Research also clearly shows that suicide is almost *always* committed in a secluded, isolated place around no one else. Those who experience depression and suicidal thoughts too often isolate themselves. In this isolation, one is often tempted to believe the lie that no one can help them; no one can empathize with them or that no one can love them.

These deceptive thoughts are lies we believe that need to be fought with the truth. There are people in this world who can help, can empathize with you and those who do deeply love you. The apostle Paul commands believers to *Bear one another's burdens, and so fulfill the law of Christ* (Galatians 6:2).

Christ-followers are told to *bear up under* and help carry the struggles and hardships of others, and that includes helping those who battle depression and suicidal thoughts. This is a command—it is not an option or a hardship; it is an opportunity for Christians to walk alongside someone (you) in a time of struggle. However, others can't help you or walk beside you if you isolate yourself from them, and if you do not inform them about your true thoughts and feelings.

Granted, other believers can't fix all your problems, and they aren't commanded to do that. The command is to help *you* carry *your* burden—to lighten your load. If you feel alone, it is tempting even to blame yourself, but if you are reading these words, it is not too late to ask others for help. It is *never* too late to open up about your emotions, your struggles, and your difficulties. There are people in this world willing to listen and love you.

2. This World Is NOT Better Off Without You

Just as it is common for those who struggle with depression to think that there is nobody who can help or love them, it is also tempting to believe that the world would be better off without them. People do not contemplate suicide because they believe the world does not deserve them—instead, suicidal thoughts result from a belief that others would be better if they were no longer living.

This is an absolute lie! You have value and purpose in this world. Granted, it may not feel like it at the moment, but in those dark seasons, don't trust your own thinking. Look beyond your thoughts to the truth of Scripture.

Allow the wisdom in the Bible to fuel your thoughts and emotions right now. It is tempting to let yourself drown in the muck and mire of your depression, but God was very clear that the world is not better off without you. God said, *For I know the plans I have for you, plans to prosper you and not to harm you, plans to give you hope and a future* (Jeremiah 29:11).

God has a plan for your life! No matter how much you may think or believe the world and others will be better off without you—that isn't true! Don't allow God's plans for your future to go unfulfilled. The people around you will be deeply crushed by losing you, and the world will miss out on all that God still has planned for you to do.

3. JESUS Experienced Depression Just Like You but Did Not Sin!

Yes, you read that correctly—Jesus experienced depression just like you! As Christians, we sometimes think that because Jesus is God, He couldn't have truly suffered as *we* suffer, and we convince ourselves that He doesn't fully understand what it's like to endure our trials. In essence, we think that Jesus doesn't fully relate to our struggles.

The Bible paints a completely different picture of Jesus. Yes, Jesus is God, but the Bible also makes it very clear that Jesus was also fully man. Jesus got hungry like a man, got tired like a man, and even bled like a man on more than one occasion. In his humanity, Jesus endured everything we could possibly imagine.

Scripture says *we do not have a high priest who is unable to empathize with our weaknesses, but we have one who has been tempted in every way, just as we are—yet he did not sin* (Hebrews 4:15). Everything you have endured, Jesus endured it as well, and He did it in His full humanity.

In fact, on the night He was betrayed by one of His disciples, Judas Iscariot, Jesus prayed. His disciples were exhausted as was Jesus, but Jesus could not sleep, just one of the many classic symptoms of depression and anxiety. On that night, the Scriptures tell us about what Jesus prayed, *And being in agony, he prayed more earnestly; and his sweat became like great drops of blood falling down to the ground* (Luke 22:44).

There is a medical term for the sweating of blood called hematohidrosis. It is an incredibly rare medical phenomenon, but almost all experts agree that other than extremely high blood pressure, the root cause of it can be intense anxiety, stress, and fear.

Think for a moment about all of Jesus' struggles. A person He chose to be a disciple betrayed Him. The disciples He loved so much and were closest to Him fell asleep when He asked them to stay alert and pray. He knew that in a short while, He would be lied about, disgraced, beaten, and ultimately crucified alone. These heavy feelings were real and carried real impacts on Jesus physically, emotionally, and spiritually.

So, it would be wrong to think that Jesus did not experience depression, anxiety, and fear. Jesus felt every human emotion you, and I feel and perhaps to a greater extent. He was, after all, 100% human, just as you and I are 100% human. As humans, we experience emotions that drive us to question everything about ourselves, our world, and even God Himself. Just because Jesus experienced *all* these emotions without sin does *not* imply that He did not truly experience the burden associated with them. Jesus' burden was real, and His emotions were intense just as yours are.

Ponder on that, and don't ever forget it in times of depression—Jesus felt what you are feeling and more. It is not a sin to experience depression, anxiety, or fear, for each of those emotions is completely human.

Nonetheless, in those moments of depression, find comfort in knowing that Jesus endured those very same emotions. Jesus did not suffer so that you would not have to suffer—He suffered so that you could know He suffers *with* you, but through His suffering, He remained sinless. Hebrews 4:15 says, ...*yet he did not sin,* and suicide would be a sin.

Conclusion...A New Day is Coming!

The Bible is clear that regardless of temporary, momentary feelings, everyone has value and bears the image of God, the purpose of God, and the love of God. This is what sets us apart from animals.

So, in your moments of depression when everything seems to be caving in, and you find yourself losing the will to face another day, remember the truth that surrounds you. You are valuable to God, even if you don't think anyone else sees it. You have a purpose in this world, even if it seems like you are wandering aimlessly. And finally, God loves you, even if it seems like no one else does.

You can, just as so many others have before you, rebound from your deepest depression and darkest moments unless you quit and give up the fight. Ending your life makes sure that you will never get better or make a positive turn. Going forward, you do not have to be perfect—no one is. The most important focus for you right now is to keep going. The sun will come up in the morning, and you need to be here to see it and celebrate this truth found in Scripture.

Isaiah 58:8, *Then your light will break forth like the dawn, and your healing will quickly appear; then your* *righteousness will go before you, and the glory of the Lord will be <u>your</u> rear guard."*

Helping During Desperate Times—If You Know Someone Contemplating Suicide

In this chapter, I want to provide insights into this deep heart-wrenching issue of depression and suicidal thinking. Both statistical data and practical counseling are relevant and fitting for helping others in desperate times.

Suicide is an unsettling issue because it is a deeply *personal* issue. Statistics concerning suicide are not mere data points on a chart or table—they are statistics about real people with real names with real struggles. These numbers are our friends, family, neighbors, and coworkers. Bringing in this statistical data is not merely informing you, but enabling you to help. While no suicide is fully understandable, and the causes are rarely clear cut, understanding the main causes and triggers can help better identify those who are particularly at risk and how we can help.

Statistics on Suicide

1. Statistics Related to All Ages

When it comes to the data concerning suicide, the statistics are always disturbing, no matter the context. The fact that Americans take their own lives to the point that it ranks in the top ten causes of death is deeply disturbing. The vast majority of our population has been touched by suicide in some way; this reality in America should cause us to weep.

The Ethics and Religious Liberty Commission (ERLC), which is an arm of the Southern Baptist Convention (SBC) devoted to engaging the culture on a variety of issues with the Gospel and the theology of the SBC, the data on suicide is jarring. From a 2014 article on "Suicide from a Christian Perspective," they note that there were roughly 29,000 suicides in 2014.

However, in 2018, the CDC released incredibly tragic data, noting that the number of suicides had climbed to a total of 44,965. This makes suicide, as of the most recent data, the tenth leading cause of death in America for all ages. To think of this reality is incredibly sobering and shows that we have much work to do when it comes to both understanding and preventing suicide in our country. Furthermore, according to the ERLC, "females are more likely to attempt suicide; however, males are four times more likely to successfully commit suicide."

Recently, as an example, a high-profile pastor named Jarrid Wilson took his own life at the age of 30. Wilson was a pastor at Harvest Church under Greg Laurie. He openly struggled with mental illness and founded an organization called "Anthem of Hope," which is dedicated to helping those struggling with anxiety and depression. His passion for ministry, coupled with the truth he knew about Jesus and the love offered by his family, was not enough to keep him from taking his own life.

Writing on Wilson's death, Ericka Andersen notes how pastors can be helped when struggling with these suicidal thoughts, but her writing applies to all professions and people:

"Faith is by no means the only pathway to hope and healing for those who struggle. The Suicide Prevention Hotline may not pray with callers, but they are there for everyone who needs them. Sadly, pastors may feel uncomfortable attending non-faith-based support groups or seeking outside counsel because they fear being found out or manifest guilt that their faith isn't enough. But, more awareness about the pressures of depression and anxiety among faith leaders, better resources aimed specifically toward them, and destigmatizing mental healthcare for this demographic will go a long way. Perhaps efforts of this kind would have been the safety net Jarrid Wilson needed to prevent his tragic end."

All people—young or old, male or female, people of color and white alike— need to know that anxiety, depression, and suicidal thoughts should always be taken seriously. If you or someone you know has received ridicule for experiencing anxiety or depression, know that it was wrong, hurtful, and evil. There is *always* someone who can and will help.

2. Statistics Related to Teens and Young Adults

The most jarring statistic concerning American adolescents and young adults is that suicide is the second-leading cause of death for those in the age range of 10-24. This is a heart-breaking statistic considering the fact that among all ages, suicide is the tenth leading cause of death. That means that it is statistically more likely for a teenager to die from suicide than homicide, cancer, and a host of other causes we fear so much. Suicide is a real problem for the young.

This crippling data proves that intervention is greatly needed because suicide is increasingly rising. Now, more than ever, teens and adolescents struggle with anxiety and depression. Suicide is a real, tangible, and clinical problem in our teens and young adults—and it is cause for deep and great concern.

If you are the parent or guardian of a teenager, or if you work with teenagers in some fashion, you are on the front lines of this battle. You see the warning signs and the triggering speech that leads you to consider a teen at risk, and you know that frequently, teens who make suicidal threats are labeled "attention seekers," as if their words have no meaning and are simply a ploy on other peoples' emotions. On this, the Lucile Packard Children's Hospital at Stanford University writes:

> *"Threats of suicide are a cry for help. Always take such statements, thoughts, behaviors, or plans very seriously. Any teen who expresses thoughts of suicide should not be left alone and should be evaluated right away...Any teen who has tried to commit suicide needs a physical checkup first to rule out life-threatening health problems. He or she should then get a mental health evaluation and treatment until he or she is stable."*

The data also shows that teen suicide is on the rise and does not seem to be slowing. Stephanie Doupnik, a writer for *Vox*, cites the CDC's data from 2018, showing that young adult suicide spiked in 1994 at 13.6 per 100,000—then it dipped over the following decade until 2007 when the rates started to climb again. Now, we sit at 14.5 suicides per 100,000 in 2017.

Doupnik, a pediatrician and child health advocate, also writes about how social media is often perceived as a cause of teen anxiety and depression, yet she argues it is more of a trigger toward a deeper depression that already exists:

> *"People often ask me how social media and the internet contribute to teenagers' risk of suicide. The teens we spoke with rarely discussed them alone as a trigger for their suicidal thoughts. However, for already vulnerable adolescents, technology*

can provide a forum for more trauma, worsening conflict or isolation. Further, having easy access to information on the Internet about how to engage in self-harm can be dangerous for teens with mental health concerns."

If you know someone who battles thoughts of harming himself or herself, assist them in finding the help needed to survive and heal. As our culture has grown to recognize the validity of mental illness and the importance of treatment, no cry for help should be ignored; no occasion to help should be overlooked.

Being a teenager and a young adult is difficult, and a helper's job is to encourage those who are hurting not to retreat from others because matters will only get worse. It is easy for those struggling with suicidal thoughts to pull back from other real relationships and only interact with the world through social media or online. As the person advising or helping someone walk through thoughts of taking his/her life, take all thoughts seriously, never stigmatize, and always remind the individual who is struggling, they are not alone. Peers, mentors, and health professionals are available.

Counseling for Those Struggling with Suicidal Thoughts

Without a doubt, those statistics and others are alarming; however, statistics are not determiners of anyone's future, but they are snapshots of the other's past. Up until the moment a person takes his or her own life, there is still hope and you *can* help them make the right choice. There is always an opportunity for change, progress, and victory. No situation should be considered 'an inevitable case,' and no life is not worth living.

Three Practical Suggestions:

1. Get Professional and Church Help

If someone is struggling with suicidal thoughts, encourage and help them to get professional help. The professional and medical community can be invaluable in those crisis moments. None of us are adequately trained to spot all the signs and see all the contributing factors that lead one to thoughts, and even desires for suicide. Nor can any of us outside of the professional community treat any underlying medial or chemical factors that lead to suicidal thoughts.

Beyond that, a local church staff likely knows or has recommendations for trusted mental health professionals who can offer professional help. The church may even have a list of licensed Christian counselors who have seen many cases similar to their present situation. A church staff will help you as much as it is able—yet it is important to remember that there are limits to every pastor or staff member's ability.

Local church staff and volunteers can't legally prescribe medication if necessary, and they cannot successfully diagnose a mental illness or lack thereof. Yet they can offer love and support to those in need and direct you to someone who can give you needed help and advice.

The Bible tells us that there is wisdom in seeking the advice and counsel of multiple people. So as you assist those who are hurting, get as much wise counsel and advice as you can. The book of Proverbs says, *Where there is no guidance, a people falls, but in an abundance of counselors, there is safety* (Proverbs 11:14). It also reminds, *for by wise guidance you can wage your war, and in abundance of counselors there is victory* (Proverbs 24:6). There is absolutely nothing wrong with seeking professional help beyond your local church staff for those with suicidal thoughts—indeed, it may be wrong for you NOT to do so! But do seek professional help.

2. Know the Difference Between Mental and Spiritual Depression

When we think of depression, our minds tend to gravitate toward the kind of depression that might be labeled "mental" or "clinical" depression. Depression is a disorder of the brain, resulting in everything from a loss of desire or interest in former hobbies to suicidal thoughts. Clinical depression is on the far end of the spectrum of the most severe status of mental depression. In those cases, there is good reason to seek medical and psychiatric treatment in the form of therapy and medication.

However, for the Christian, there must be the recognition that there is a difference between mental and spiritual depression. Spiritual depression is the depression of not merely the mind but the soul. Spiritual depression consists of feelings of spiritual hopelessness and fatigue, perhaps even slipping into the belief that God is either absent or ambivalent about life's problems. Many even drift to the far extreme and announce belief that there is no God at all. Usually, these thoughts stem from the lack of Scripture intake, prayer, fellowship with other believers, and distancing oneself from the local church.

In his deeply pastoral work, *Spiritual Depression: Its Causes and Cure*, Martyn Lloyd-Jones writes that the true cause of all spiritual depression is simply unbelief:

> *"Indeed, I can put it, finally, like this; the ultimate cause of spiritual depression is unbelief. For if it were not for unbelief even the devil could do nothing. It is because we listen to the devil instead of listening to God that we go down before him and fall before his attacks. That is why the psalmist keeps on saying to himself: 'Hope thou in God for I shall yet praise Him...' He reminds himself of God. Why? Because he was depressed and had forgotten God, so that his faith and his belief in God and in God's power, and in his relationship to God, were not what they ought to be. We can indeed sum it all up by saying that the final and ultimate cause is just sheer unbelief."*

In moments of depression and anxiety, the temptation for the one struggling is to isolate from others, to shirk obedience to God in His Word, and to run, like Jonah, in the complete opposite direction of God's will and God's people. Yet spiritual depression has its cure, and that cure is Jesus, the One who endured everything we have, yet without sin. So as a helper, you must know the difference between mental and spiritual depression, and both need to be treated accordingly. Mental depression needs to be treated by those in the medical field while spiritual depression is best treated by those who love and serve God. Don't ever forget, the God who created our brain and emotions is also the one who saves and redeems them by His Grace.

3. Run to Jesus, His Word, and His Church

When helping people who battle depression, offer accountability and assistance with getting them back into Scripture, church, and prayer. Encourage and partner with them in praying about their situation and seeking God's wisdom and direction. Seeking out professional help is absolutely the right advice when dealing with dark, depressive suicidal thoughts, but do not ignore the help that is found in Jesus Christ, His Word, and His Church.

There is no set formula for when to seek professional help and when to lean heavily on spiritual help. I think it is important to realize that both are vitally important when people are deeply struggling. If you are walking along-side a family member, a friend, a coworker, or a fellow church member who is a believer, help them remember this above all things: they are infinitely loved by the God who created them, and His Son who gave His life for them, and sustains them so that *their* life can and will find fulfillment again. Jesus said, *The thief comes only to steal and kill and destroy. I came that they may have life and have it abundantly* (John 10:10).

There are certain comforts JESUS gives those who are hurting that the world cannot offer. As Jesus was leaving His disciples to go to the cross, He left them with peace: *Peace I leave with you; my peace I give you. I do not give to you as the world gives. Do not let your hearts be troubled and do not be afraid* (John 14:27). There is comfort in this world that can help in dark moments, but nothing in this world offers the life and peace that Jesus can. Encourage them to run to Him and find comfort and peace in Him and His people.

There are comforts in God's WORD, and in His promises to us. As has been stated earlier, the apostle Paul dealt with afflictions at every turn in his life. And when he asked for one of them to be taken away three times, the Lord refused. Instead, He reminded Paul: *But he said to me, "My grace is sufficient for you, for my power is made perfect in weakness." Therefore I will boast all the more gladly about my weaknesses, so that Christ's power may rest on me. That is why, for Christ's sake, I delight in weaknesses, in insults, in hardships, in persecutions, in difficulties. For when I am weak, then I am strong* (2 Corinthians 12:9-10). Paul *delighted* in his weaknesses, knowing that God would make him strong where he was weak. That is a promise for those who are struggling—just like Paul, where they are weak, God will make them stronger if they will let Him.

Finally, there are comforts in Christ's CHURCH. No church is perfect, and the people in those churches aren't perfect either. Churches are filled with people who have gone through tough seasons and other people who are still going through tough seasons. The psalmist writes in Psalm 94:19, *When anxiety was great within me, your consolation brought me joy.* God has given us His people, the church to be part of that consoling process. Other broken and hurting people can help. There are people who have struggled with the same anxieties, depression, and thoughts that the one you are working with has and they can bring encouragement. Help the person you are working with, find that consolation and comfort in the church, knowing that the people in the church are there to *carry each other's burdens, and in this way you will fulfill the law of Christ* (Galatians 6:2).

Conclusion

I know that a short chapter is probably not going to be the cure-all for someone's depression. After reading this, there are likely still thoughts swirling in your head like how do I help them deal with the temptation to keep thinking the world will be better off without them. Just keep reminding them those are lies. And the truths to fight these lies are found in the Father of all Truth, His Son, and the Holy Spirit.

If the one you are working with is a Christian, the Holy Spirit *lives* in them. If they are not a Christian or if you are unsure, seek out a pastor, staff member for direction on helping them find the peace that can us only found in accepting Jesus as Savior and Lord. Remind them, that they will never stop struggling with sin on this side of eternity, but they can have victory over the thoughts that plague them. God may sovereignly heal them of all these ailing thoughts, but whether He does or not, He is always good and will carry them to victory.

Remind them when they feel hopeless, there is still hope. If they feel worthless, there is worthiness in them. If they feel rejected, hated, or even alone—there is love for them. And all of these things, if they cannot find them in any other person, will be found in Jesus. Encourage them to run to Him in all things, for all things, and through all things. For in Him, there is abundant *life!* Read the Apostles Prayer for the Ephesians believers, and pray this over and for the one who is hurting:

> **Ephesians 3:16,** *I pray that out of his glorious riches he may strengthen you with power through his Spirit in your inner being, [17]so that Christ may dwell in your hearts through faith. And I pray that you, being rooted and established in love, [18]may have power, together with all the Lord's holy people, to grasp how wide and long and high and deep is the love of Christ, [19]and to know this love that surpasses knowledge...*

Healing and Hope After Suicide

This book has covered some weighty issues concerning the realities of suicide, including ways believers can battle against suicide and the depression that may cause it, yet you may be reading this book for an entirely different reason. Maybe *you* are not struggling with depression or suicidal thoughts, but you find yourself trying to understand how and why someone might arrive at the point of self-harm or suicide. Possibly you have lost a family member, friend, coworker, neighbor, student, community leader... and you can't comprehend the ending of a life unnecessarily cut short.

You are stuck on the WHY. You are mad at the lost time with this person. You are sad about the absence of future impact, memories, and accomplishments of life without the one who took his or her life. You realize that the lost one chose a permanent, life-ending solution to a temporary though significant hurdle. And, you can't get past the WHY.

Perhaps you are reading this book not out of a desire for hope, but for answers. Maybe a loved one in your life committed suicide, leaving you and others behind to mourn, grieve, and question. You may be battling questions of whether or not you did enough to prevent their death, whether or not you were to blame, or whether or not God forgives a person for suicide. You may even experience resentment and anger at their selfish, short-sighted decision that carried such a permanent result.

In her book *Finding Your Way after the Suicide of Someone You Love*, co-written with David Biebel, Suzanne Foster recounts the moment she and her husband found the body of their daughter: "It was all very strange. She had a smile on her face. Her body was warm. But her color was wrong, very wrong."[1] She goes on to write about the pain and questions that can surface almost immediately, but never truly go away in the mind of someone who loses someone they love to suicide:

"A survivor of suicide is anyone who has been affected by the loss of someone to suicide—parent, spouse, child, sibling, or friend. 'It's an exclusive club I joined without wanting to,' one survivor told us. 'But I passed the initiation so I guess I'm a member.' Following a loved one's suicide, many questions haunt the survivors, the most common of which start with why, such as: Why did my loved one choose death over life? Why didn't I see it coming? Similar questions are common to other

1 David B. Biebel and Suzanne L. Foster, *Finding Your Way after the Suicide of Someone You Love*, (Grand Rapids: Zondervan, 2005).

losses...When a loved one's death was self-inflicted, however, some of the questions that linger the longest relate to the one who has died."[2]

The Bible is crucial to healing. Seeking out Scripture for wisdom, comfort, and direction helps those of us who have experienced the trauma of the suicide of a loved one. Scripture prevents bogging yourself down in wrong thinking that often occurs in the grieving process.

What Does Scripture Teach About Suicide?

It is important to know that God *hears* your questions, and He *cares* about them, but He does not *always* answer them. Some questions encountered during the process of grief will go unanswered; however, comfort can be found in the answers God *gives* us in His Word, knowing that He has not left us alone in the darkness of our grief.

Scripture does not give a simple step-by-step list explaining what happened to those who committed suicide. It does not offer advice on how to prevent this loss from happening again, nor does it explain why some people end up choosing suicide when others do not. However, it *does* discuss some accounts of people who did commit suicide, the effect it had on others, and ways to combat wrong thinking surrounding suicide.

---

2 Ibid.

1. Is Suicide an Unpardonable Sin?

When grieving the loss of life as a result of suicide, the grief can be heart-wrenching. One question that haunts many is: Did the one who ended his or her own life go to Heaven or Hell? Loved ones may question whether those who commit suicide can still be with the Lord. Can the person who claimed to be a Christian still be forgiven for taking their own life?

Some have argued or assumed through church history that suicide is an unpardonable sin. The reason for this is because suicide immediately removes the possibility of confession and repentance. This leaves suicide survivors in a state of anxiety, wondering if their departed loved ones are possibly separated from God.

In Roman Catholic theology, for example, sin is removed through the sacraments of penance and confession. Catholic theology also distinguishes between mortal (sins that separate a person from their salvation) and venial sins (sins that can be forgiven). Because suicide is a mortal sin, the state of the person's soul in eternity is thrown into jeopardy, leaving those who loved the deceased in a state of anxiety and concern.

Scripture does not teach that suicide is a mortal sin. We know that repentance is indeed required for the forgiveness of sins (1 John 1:9; Luke 24:46). Yet we also know that the death of Jesus Christ provided *eternal* and *perfect* forgiveness for *all* sins, even those for which we have not specifically confessed (John 6:37, 10:28, Romans 5:1-10, 8:37-39; Hebrews 10:8-14; Psalm 103:11-12).

Therefore, even though suicide *is* murder, and all murder is sin, this does *not* mean that a Christian who commits suicide is in danger of God's eternal wrath. For *all* of God's wrath was poured out on Jesus in our place, so that no matter what we do, we can rest assured we will be with Jesus for eternity (2 Corinthians 5:21).

If you are struggling with doubt and questions concerning your loved one's suicide, be encouraged by knowing that where they are now is not determined by good or bad decisions, including the choice of how they ended life. Your loved one's suicide does not mean they did not trust God, or that they lost their faith. Where your loved one is now was determined by their acceptance of God's love and Jesus' sacrifice for sin on the cross at Calvary. God's love is greater than suicide and reaches beyond the grave for His children.

2. How should I feel after the tragedy of suicide?

Another question someone may wrestle with after the suicide of a loved one is: how should I feel after such a devastating event. Of course, grief is expected, but for how long? Does God expect us to "get over it" quickly? Should Christians be able to move on quicker than non-Christians? Does prolonged grief become sinful? After all, throughout Scripture, God instructs Christians to rejoice always and find joy in the Lord. So how does Scripture teach us to *feel* after the suicide of a loved one?

Scripture is not entirely silent on suicide—indeed, it gives us some accounts of suicide, as was covered earlier in this work. We think of Samson, for example, who asked the Lord for one more instance of supernatural strength so he could crush the Philistines to death along with himself (Judges 16:26-27). We also think of the suicide of Judas Iscariot, Jesus' betrayer, who killed himself out of the immense grief and regret he felt for his damning words and actions which led to the arrest and crucifixion of Christ (Matthew 27:1-10).

For the question of how to feel after losing someone to suicide, let's turn to the death of King Saul. 1 Samuel 31, shares about yet another battle between the Israelites and the Philistines. As the battle raged, Saul knew the battle was lost, especially after his son died in the battle. King Saul commanded his armor-bearer to kill him after Philistine arrows had wounded him. When the armor-bearer refused, Saul fell on his sword, killing himself.

At the time of the battle, David, who would become king in Saul's place, had been running and hiding from the murderous King Saul for years, knowing that Saul's hatred and envy of David were growing rapidly. As news of Saul's death came to David in 2 Samuel 1, one might have expected David to be thrilled and overjoyed at the fact that Saul killed himself. Yet, as David inquires about the battle:

> **2 Samuel 1:4,** *"What happened?" David asked. "Tell me." "The men fled from the battle," he replied. "Many of them fell and died. And Saul and his son Jonathan are dead."... ¹¹Then David and all the men with him*

*took hold of their clothes and tore them. ¹²They
mourned and wept and fasted till evening for Saul and
his son Jonathan, and for the army of the Lord and
for the nation of Israel, because they had fallen by the
sword.*

In ancient Israel, and throughout the Ancient Near
East, the tearing of clothing is a sign of deep mourning
and grief. David tore his clothes, as did those who accom-
panied him. Not only did they do this, but they also *wept
and fasted* for Saul and his son, Jonathan. It did not matter
to David that Saul was an enemy or that Saul had attempted to kill David. The suicide of Saul crushed David's soul
and led him into mourning for his friend and his king.

If you have experienced the loss of a loved one to suicide, your grief is not an hourglass of sand—it does not
come with a timer. God does not expect you to "get over
it" and move on in a certain time frame. The instruction
in Scripture to rejoice always and to mourn deeply can go
hand in hand, especially when we stop thinking of joy and
happiness as though they are the same. Grief comes and
goes like waves from the ocean to the beach. Everyone
grieves differently and for different amounts of time, yet
the one truth Scripture shows us is that all death, especially suicide, is personally devastating for those left behind.

Does Scripture offer Truths Concerning Grief?

In addition to Scripture speaking directly to the
topic of suicide, God's divine Word hands us advice and

wisdom concerning grief. When a loved one commits suicide, grief is inevitable and often instantaneous. Questions surrounding grief can revolve around how long it will last, how intense it will remain, or how it tends to come and go at the most seemingly random times. I desire to offer encouragement and help you navigate through the grief.

1. Is Grief a sin?

As stated above, it can be tempting to think that grieving a person's death (or grieving anything for that matter) can cause us to fall into sin. With Scripture's commands to rejoice always and to find our happiness in Christ, is it a sin when grief obsessively lingers? Does God become angry when we can't look upon a loss and move on to peace and healing? Does a long period of grief show a lack of faith or spiritual maturity?

Scripture is clear that grief is not sinful, no matter how long or how intense it may be. One common element that those in mourning often have is the intermittent heavy, spontaneous onset of sadness. Simple, daily tasks like cooking dinner, watching sports, or even something as innocuous as a particular traffic light trigger the grief all over again.

In Psalm 6, King David wrote about a time in his life where he was in deep, desperate need of God's grace. We do not know exactly what moment was causing David's such intense grief, but we do know there were many occasions in David's life when such grief would have been understandable. He writes:

Psalm 6:6-7, *I am worn out from my groaning. All night long I flood my bed with weeping and drench my couch with tears. ⁷My eyes grow weak with sorrow.*

King David was not sinning in his grief. Indeed, as a man after God's own heart, he proved to be acting righteously by bringing his grief before God. Grief may be the very emotion that *brings* us to God and other believers and saves us from its debilitating effects. Nevertheless, this deep sorrow caused by someone's death is deeply painful, and the physical, emotional, and spiritual impacts of prolonged grief are difficult to bear for sure.

In addition to King David's example of the reality that grief is not sinful, our sinless Savior experienced intense grief in John 11, when Jesus was informed that his friend, Lazarus, had died. Scripture says that Jesus was *deeply moved in spirit and troubled* and that *Jesus wept* (John 11:33, 35). Those expressions carry the idea of both an internal and external deep sense of mourning, grief and loss. Jesus' grief was both internal and invisible to others along with external and visible to those around Him.

In Gethsemane, Jesus spoke with His remaining disciples after Judas Iscariot had left to betray Him. As Jesus attempted to pray, taking His inner circle of Peter, James, and John with Him, He said, *My soul is overwhelmed with sorrow to the point of death. Stay here and keep watch with me.* (Matthew 26:38)

Jesus Himself was overwhelmed and grief-stricken. He felt as if He could die from the thought of His own impending death that caused such grief. What a comfort it is to know that Jesus Christ, the Son of God Himself, grieved to a point where He was inconsolable, just like those of us who have experienced the suicide of a loved one, yet His overwhelming grief was not a sin—He *never* sinned!

2. Will Grief Go Away?

For those people who have endured the suicide of a loved one, the grief may truly never go away, or certainly, it will remain for a long time. In 2 Corinthians 12:1-10, the apostle Paul tells the Corinthians about his "thorn in the flesh." We do not know what this "thorn" was. We do not know if it was a physical sickness, emotional or even a spiritual disposition of grief he may have had. Yet whatever this thorn was, it caused Paul deep and constant grief leading Paul to cry out to the Lord *three times* asking for it to be removed.

Each time Paul prayed for the thorn to be removed, God said, "No, No, and No." Even the apostle Paul, as righteous and godly as he was, received God's "no." He writes:

2 Corinthians 12:8, *Three times I pleaded with the Lord to take it away from me. ⁹But he said to me, "My grace is sufficient for you, for my power is made perfect in weakness." Therefore I will boast all the more gladly about my weaknesses, so that Christ's power may rest on me. ¹⁰That is why, for Christ's sake, I delight in weaknesses, in insults, in hardships, in persecutions, in difficulties. For when I am weak, then I am strong.*

Paul's pain and grief did not go away. Nevertheless, Paul did *not* grow angry or resentful toward God. He knew that through this suffering, God was using Paul's pain to prove that only grace sustains and supports him. Sometimes, God uses our grief and suffering to draw us closer to Him, His power, and His grace. In fact, Paul found out that that pain and weakness became a central strength of his life and ministry.

Your grief may be taken away tomorrow, or next week, or next year, or never. Yet, in every case, God's grace is sufficient for you. Accordingly, having God's grace in your life is infinitely better than *not* having the grief in your life. So as you make your journey through the grief of losing a loved one, be assured that that weakness will become a strength and an opportunity to minister to someone else in the days ahead.

3. Should my grief be shared by others?

Scripture teaches that grief should be shared by others. Jesus said, *Blessed are those who mourn, for they will be comforted* (Matthew 5:4). However, comfort cannot come in isolation. Since comfort means to soothe, console, or bring cheer to someone, by definition, it requires at least two people.

Grief is an isolating emotion, causing us to be introspective and contemplative about the loved ones we've lost. Too often, people who grieve keep themselves isolated and alone, as if no one else could possibly understand or help them.

Consider the prophet Elijah. After he demonstrated the faithfulness of the Lord to the entire nation of Israel, the king's ungodly wife, Jezebel, sought to have him killed. Elijah was on the run from Jezebel and sought shelter in the wilderness alone. In his grief, Elijah prayed to the Lord:

> **1 Kings 19:3**, *Elijah was afraid and ran for his life. When he came to Beersheba in Judah, he left his servant there, ⁴while he himself went a day's journey into the wilderness. He came to a broom bush, sat down under it and prayed that he might die. "I have had enough, Lord," he said. "Take my life; I am no better than my ancestors." ⁵Then he lay down under the bush and fell asleep.*

Jonah was another prophet who experienced such an intense amount of grief. After he preached against the city of Nineveh, the entire city repented, and God showed them mercy instead of judgment. Jonah hated this fact because of his hatred for the Ninevites. His anger turned into grief, and his grief and isolation turned into a lament of life itself, so he prayed:

> **Jonah 4:2**, *He prayed to the Lord, "Isn't this what I said, Lord, when I was still at home? That is what I tried to forestall by fleeing to Tarshish. I knew that you are a gracious and compassionate God, slow to anger and abounding in love, a God who relents from sending calamity. ³Now, Lord, take away my life, for it is better for me to die than to live."*

Though the kind of grief you are experiencing after the suicide of a loved one is different than the ones expressed above, several key insights can be gleaned from the above examples. First, being alone or keeping oneself isolated from others only intensifies the grief process. Second, those examples serve as good reminders that grief itself can be so severe that it causes one to despair of even living, especially when carried alone.

However, God never intended for you or anyone else to grieve alone; instead God intended for you to be blessed and comforted by others. Yes, God can and does comfort us in our grief even when we are alone, but that is only part of the answer to overcoming your grief. The other piece of recovering from the loss of a loved one is to allow others to bless, comfort, and encourage you as well. In addition, having the support of others offers accountability for you to take positive steps to heal. So, while there are times when you need a moment to be alone with the true reality of your loss and the real changes that will follow, God never intended you to always grieve alone.

4. Can my Grief Become a Source of Help for Others?

The final, and often overlooked part of grief's recovery process, is the healing that takes place when personal pain is utilized to help others. The Apostle Paul said:

2 Corinthians 1:3, *Praise be to the God and Father of our Lord Jesus Christ, the Father of compassion*

and the God of all comfort, who comforts us in all our troubles, so that we can comfort those in any trouble with the comfort we ourselves receive from God.

Once comforted by God and others, our energy can best be spent offering support and wisdom to others who might be traveling a grief-stricken path. Even if you cannot, at this moment, conceive of helping someone else through pain, be assured that day will come if you allow your healing to take place by receiving comfort from God and others.

In the days ahead, be aware of people who are in pain. You do not have to be a trained professional to help others through grief—simply comfort them the way you longed to be comforted.

Conclusion

There is coming a day when God will:

Revelation 21:4, *'He will wipe every tear from their eyes. There will be no more death' or mourning or crying or pain, for the old order of things has passed away." ⁵He who was seated on the throne said, "I am making everything new!" Then he said, "Write this down, for these words are trustworthy and true."*

Your grief does have an expiration date when every tear will be wiped away and all crying and grief will be removed. However, until that day, remember the truths mentioned in this chapter:

- Your grief is not a sin
- Your grief may never fully go away
- You were never meant to grieve alone
- Your hurt can turn into someone else's healing.

I hope that your journey of grief is helped through the hope and comfort that is found in this truth. The truth of Scripture reminds us that suicide is not the end and that grief *does* indeed have an expiration date. For the One Who holds all the power has conquered death, the grave, and suicide—and we will one day conquer it with Him!

1 Corinthians 15:55, *"Where, O death, is your victory? Where, O death, is your sting?"* [56]*The sting of death is sin, and the power of sin is the law.* [57]*But thanks be to God! He gives us the victory through our Lord Jesus Christ.* [58]*Therefore, my dear brothers and sisters, stand firm. Let nothing move you. Always give yourselves fully to the work of the Lord, because you know that your labor in the Lord is not in vain.*

Conclusion

As a Pastor, I am very aware that one book cannot stem the rising tide of suicide. I have worked with too many suicidal individuals as well as their families to think there is one specific answer for every case. However, I have come to realize that sharing my personal experiences and the mistakes I made can help others navigate their particular journey.

I am also convinced that the more people who are aware of the realities of suicide, the better off we all are. Just like there is rarely just one cause of suicide, there is also rarely just one cure. However, the more people who can take away one or two kernels of truth from a work like this the more society and those around us will benefit. Beyond that, there are many other books and articles that are available on the subject of suicide that have been written by those who are professionals and specialists in the areas of suicide and depression. Glean what you can from this book and then find other books or articles that give you a few more bits of insight into suicide's causes and treatments.

If you are grappling with suicidal thoughts, I assure you there are many good reasons for you to choose life. Yes, it takes courage to live on in the face of your discouragement and doubt, but courageously choosing to live is always preferable to death. Get the help you need from professionals and don't isolate yourself from others. God created you as a relational being and if you distance yourself from others, you are prone to feel more hopeless. Being with God's people and the Church is vital to your restorative progress.

If you have a friend or family member who is wrestling with suicidal feelings, don't ever give up on them. Also, don't believe you have to or even can solve their problem alone. Point them to professional assistance from the medical community, then help them get connected or reconnected to a church. It is in the Church that the person you are working with will be reminded of the hope of God and their purpose in life on a weekly basis.

Finally, if like me, you have lost a loved one to suicide, I'm beyond sorry! The grief you now experience at some level was almost too much for me. It was definitely too much for me to carry alone. But as you navigate your healing process, look for others around you who you can help on their journey. Honestly, writing this book was one of the hardest things I've ever done, but knowing that I might be able to help just one person in the process has made it all worth it. After all, helping others traverse a path you have been down yourself is part of the healing process.

Jeremiah 29:11, *"For I know the plans I have for you,"*
declares the Lord, "plans to prosper you and not to
harm you, plans to give you hope and a future.[12] *Then*
you will call on me and come and pray to me, and I
will listen to you. [13] *You will seek me and find me when*
you seek me with all your heart. [14] *I will be found by*
you," declares the Lord, "and will bring you back from
captivity."

Sincerely,
John Mark Caton, Ph.D.

CPSIA information can be obtained
at www.ICGtesting.com
Printed in the USA
BVHW092140070220
571816BV00005B/8